The Coming Of Hester

Jean Katherine Baird

THE COMING OF HESTER

BY

JEAN K. BAIRD

ILLUSTRATED BY ARTHUR O. SCOTT

1909

BOSTON

LOTHROP, LEE & SHEPARD CO.

Published, August, 1909.

Norwood Press
J. S. Cushing Co. — Berwick & Smith Co.
Norwood, Mass., U.S.A.

SHE LOOKED PROFESSOR SANDERSON SQUARELY IN THE FACE.
Page 104.

ILLUSTRATIONS

v

THE COMING OF HESTER

CHAPTER I

DEBBY ALDEN was hanging out the last piece of the weekly wash. It was not yet eight o'clock, but Debby was not one to be slack about her work. She hated "slop" work, as she termed washing, to hang on until the middle of the morning, so she was out of bed at daylight and about it. She was a tall, slender woman, with clear-cut features inclined toward being sharp. She was wiry and quick of movement, with a voice that carried far when she put it to use; which was not frequent, for she was a woman of few words. She was strong in her likes and dislikes and fearless in the expression of her opinion. She was independent in thought and action, no one in her little world being able to force his opinion upon her.

1

She was a woman of good judgment, with a large fund of practical common sense which so far had never failed her. Her mind had not received a great amount of culture, but it was keen in its perceptions, and logical in its reasoning. Had she been a man, she might have been a criminal lawyer or a great financier. She had a fine appreciation of humor, although she herself was far from being humorous. She was more inclined toward a sarcastic wit, which stood her in need when curiously inclined neighbors ventured too far upon her private domains.

She had sprung from a long line of thrifty, honest, unpretentious, plain-speaking folk, and she was the epitome of all her forebears.

Her manner was undemonstrative — almost stern. If affection or love made a part of her composition, she kept them well in the background, and only a few who really understood her knew the depths of sacrifice and devotion of which her love was capable.

Her house, though barren of any suggestion of luxuries or articles of finer taste, was the picture of cleanliness and good sense. She had everything needed for her comfort and convenience. Her furniture was old-fashioned, but well-kept and utilitarian. She saw no reason to discard an excellent article because present fashions declared it out of date.

Her logical mind showed itself in her dress as it did in her house. Her dark wrapper was whole and clean, and quite short enough to escape the ground. Her sleeves were rolled above the elbow, and the front of her dress was protected by a large apron of blue and white check. Her great mass of brown hair was braided tightly and wound about her head until it looked like a crown. There was a suggestion of waves about it, but she kept it so tightly braided that the waves never went further than a suggestion.

When the last article had been hung plumb and straight on the line, Debby took up her basket preparatory to returning to the wash-house. But the morning appealed to her. She paused to draw in a breath of air and to look about her.

A choice of views was before her. Near at hand was her own little place, too small to be called a farm, yet large enough to provide her living for her. There was her early garden with hotbeds for the young plants; her field of sweet corn, and to the left of this, an acre laid out in potatoes.

Then close at hand was the great rambling old house built to hold a large family; and before this was the yard with its grass plots, its beds of flowers, and the old-fashioned shrubs and plants which her grandmother had placed there. It was a peaceful scene. She gave a sigh of contentment as her eyes rested upon it.

At the edge of the place and across the public road were the signs of the noise and hurry of business life. A half-dozen tracks of railroad came together here. The public driveway crossed them almost at right angles, and ascended a steep hill, where it cut out its course close to the foot of the mountain — a dangerous position, with the rocky barriers on one side and the railroad on the outer edge — a hundred feet below.

Less than a mile away was another wall of mountains, at whose foot the river ran like a hem to the great skirt of green. In the valley between, rose the smoke and noise from the great railroad shops where hundreds of men worked day after day, and year after year, to keep the engines and cars ready to carry their great traffic of lives and freight.

The stir and bustle of this view did not please her. Her people had been quiet, rural folk, and from them she inherited a taste for the old homestead and pastoral life.

There had been a large family of them, but one by one they had gone their way, until she alone kept up the old place. She had not found her life a lonely one, for she had had no scenes of gayety with which to compare it. She had attended the country school until she had conquered the "large" arithmetic, the "big" geography, and had worked a few examples in algebra. She had had her season of sleigh-rides, spelling schools, and taffy pulls. But when she had reached the twenties and was yet Miss Debby, she dropped from this social life, for it was the custom of this country-side that a spinster of twenty-five should be retired from active social life.

With the sleigh-rides and taffy pulls and spelling-bees went her smart dressing and fluffy hair and little fixings of the toilette dear to the heart of a belle.

She had but passed her twenty-fifth birthday, yet to an indifferent observer she appeared much older, for although her hair was as brown and satiny as the inside of the ripe chestnut burr, and her face as unwrinkled as a child's, the rigid straight lines of her dressing brought into relief all

the angles of her form and features, robbing
her of every girlish grace.

After a few minutes of contemplation,
she aroused herself to the present. "Standing so when my tubs are not emptied and
the wash-house is yet to be scrubbed!"

Turning about quickly, she walked briskly
back to the house. A neighbor sat on the
wash-house steps, a folded newspaper in
her hand.

"Why, Kate Bowerman! how did you
ever slip in without my hearing you? Why
didn't you call?"

"I wasn't in a hurry. I peeped in here,
and, seeing your tubs standing, supposed you
were hanging out. You're late to-day. I was
all hung out and scrubbed out an hour ago."

"I'd been, too, but I washed some spreads,
and the blankets that were on my bed.
Blankets take so many rinsings. But, somehow, this summer the nights get so cold I
can't sleep comfortably without them.
There's always a dampness from the river."

"You coddle yourself too much. The nights have been none too cool. Blankets from the first day of October to the first of May is my rule, and I keep to it. Blankets in one day and out the next hain't my way. It's too slack."

"I'm going by no rules as long as the weather don't. It's reasonable to suppose the nights will be at least comfortable from the last of May to the middle of September. That's what folks used to count on. But there's no telling any more. As long as the weather has no laws, I hain't having none about using blankets."

Her guest laughed. Yet the result of her facial contortions could scarcely be graced by such a name. It was a mirthless cackle in which ill humors and ugly spirit were manifest. Her voice was sharp and so accustomed to ill-natured speech that even her well-meant words savored of malice and ill feeling.

Debby went on about her work, emptying

her tubs as she continued the conversation.
She was wondering why Mrs. Bowerman
had seen fit to run over at this unusual hour
of the day. She knew that some reason lay
behind the visit; it was not mere chance.
She saw the paper in her caller's hand, and
rightfully supposed it held some relation to
the visit, but she would not have asked for
the world.

Mrs. Bowerman chatted of indifferent
matters for some moments, and then said
abruptly, "I suppose you are wondering
why I ran over Monday morning?"

"No, I'm not."

"You seemed so absent-minded, I took it
for granted you were trying to think why I
came."

"I was wondering whether I'd have fruit-
cake or raisin pie for dinner. I'm a little
uncertain about the fruit-cake. I'm afraid
it won't hold out until I make more."

"Shouldn't put it on for every Tom, Dick,
and Harry that comes in. I set my table

according to the people that eat at it. There's only a few get fruit-cake."

Now, deep in her heart, Debby Alden approved of such theories, but never had she carried them into practice. It was not her way to commend any of the theories or plans of Mrs. Bowerman. She hung up her tubs in silence and took down the mop from its place on the wall of the wash-house.

Mrs. Bowerman, feeling that nothing could be gained by further reticence, held out the folded paper, saying, as she did so, "I saw an item in last night's paper which I knew you'd prick up your ears at."

"You talk as though I was a badly broken colt."

"It's about a friend of yours." Here Mrs. Bowerman gave her malicious laugh. "It says that Doctor James K. Baker has gone to Europe for a three months' visit. There's a long piece about him. It seems that he's been overworking, and his congregation gave him this trip as a present."

"That's nice." Debby's lips were closed tightly as she made a strenuous effort to insert the cleaning rag into the clasps of the mop.

"It's too bad you and him didn't make it up. It would have been a nice trip for you. Of course, his congregation wouldn't have sent one without the other."

"You're talking about something you don't know anything about, Kate. You've bothered yourself a good deal about me lately with your wondering and guessing. Now I'll tell you the truth right here, and it will save you asking any more questions. Jim Baker and I never quarrelled. We never had anything to make up about. He took me sleigh-riding a few times when we went to school. That was all. He came here to visit after he'd gone through college. But why shouldn't he? If he hadn't have come, the folks would all have been saying that he was thinking himself better than the rest of us, and had slighted us dreadfully.

Jim Baker and I are as good friends as we always were, and there's not a man in this country I admire as much. I'm glad he's getting along. I hope he always will. He's worked hard for all he's getting, and he deserves every bit of it. Take that home with you, Kate. It will set you thinking and give you something to talk about."

By this time her mop had been properly adjusted, and she fell to work upon the floor with an unnecessary expenditure of energy.

Kate stuck out her tongue — a little mannerism of hers which was far from pleasing — and laughed scornfully.

"What a fuss to make over nothing. I say something jokingly, and you fly at me as though I had been insulting you. There must be something back of all this, or else you wouldn't be so touchy. You must feel hard on the subject, or you wouldn't fly up so." She arose from the doorway and made ready to depart. But before

going she delivered one of the old saws
of the locality, laughing scornfully as she
did so. "You know, Deb, what your
own grandmother used to say, 'It's the
"bealed" place that won't bear touching.'"
She threw the paper toward Debby. "I'll
leave the paper. You might want to read
about Jim."

"Don't bother. I know he's getting
along, and I'm not much given to par-
ticulars."

She kept close to her work with the mop,
and not so much as turned her head toward
the departing guest.

"Well, I'll leave it, anyhow. You might
think better of it." With this speech she
turned and made her way under the orchard trees to the lane which led to her own
home.

Debby worked steadily until there was
no chance of her visitor's returning. Then,
laying aside her mop, she took up the paper
and read each word of the article which told

of the departure of Doctor James Baker for
Europe, and which lauded his work above
other men of his day.

Then she folded and laid the paper away,
and went back to her work. It was not
the Alden way to day-dream or to grieve
over what had gone, and Debby, in whom
all the strongest traits of her ancestors
were epitomized, kept her emotions well
under control. She had not acknowledged
to herself how much of her interest had
been centred in the boy, Jim, of her school
days. They had been brought up together,
sharing in common each thought and pleasure. Then Jim had gone away for six
years. When he came back with the ways
of college and city, Debby was constrained
and shy. She felt ill at ease in his presence,
and treated him with a cold courtesy which
he had misunderstood.

She had not done herself justice. She
had hidden beneath her frigid manner
all the noble traits of her character. She

was brusque and scornful of tongue, and awkward in manner.

Jim had lingered about the old place for several weeks, and then went off. He had written once to her, a letter of courtesy, merely, for performing her duties of hostess in the home while he had been guest. That had been eight years before, when she was almost eighteen and he twenty-five. She had heard of his successes. But she would not acknowledge to herself or to her little world that Jim Baker held a place in her life or her thoughts.

There were neither regrets nor tears as she set about her work in the preparation of dinner. She ate alone, but prepared each meal as though there were others to partake of it. She had no tolerance for those peaky, delicate women who pieced instead of eating three substantial meals each day. She prepared her dinner of meat and vegetables, with a piece of pie for dessert. She was about to sit down when there came to her ears the sound of footsteps upon the kitchen porch. A caller at this hour was unusual. The tin pedler in search of rags and old iron was the only one who timed his visits at the midday meal. He had made his rounds but the week before, so it could not be he. She waited an instant and then went to the door, flinging it wide open with her characteristic vehemence.

The sight which met her eyes was not one to cause alarm. A young woman, exhausted by a long walk and the burden of a year-old child in her arms, was sitting on the porch steps to rest. She was older than Debby Alden, but so plump and round of face and body that she seemed but a child. She was neatly dressed in a dark skirt and white shirt-waist. Her eyes were large and dark, while her dark hair waved and curled about her face. Her skin was dark, but clear. She made a beautiful picture as she leaned against the white pillars of the porch, with the soft spray

of the wild cucumber vines swaying about
her.

The child lay asleep in her arms. Debby
Alden had been the youngest child in her
own family, and knew little of the ways of
children. She had not cared for them.
The daily sacrifices and duties of a mother
were a surprise to her. She had often
wondered how any woman could give up
her own comfort and convenience for the
welfare of a child. It was not strange,
then, that the beautiful child made no ap-
peal to her. Her quick glance rested for
a moment upon the woman and the babe,
and in an instant had grasped each detail
of face and dress. The woman at once
began an explanation. She had come on
the train which had passed an hour before.
She had mistook the trainman's words.
She thought the train had reached the
station, and she had gotten off. She had
found that the town was fully three miles
distant and that the train had stopped

merely for orders. She had no wish to disturb the lady, but the road was so hot and dusty and the sleeping child had been very heavy. She wished to rest but a moment. If the lady could give them a little to eat, — a piece of bread for herself and a glass of milk for the child, — she would be glad to pay anything within reason.

Debby Alden reared back her head haughtily. "The Aldens have not yet reached the place where they set a price for a piece of bread to a stranger. Come in." She flung wide the door. Then, with native hospitality, she took the child in her own arms and carried her into the darkened living-room, where she laid her upon the couch.

"She can have her sleep out," she said, returning to the kitchen. "She can have her milk when she gets awake. You can't go on in the heat of the day."

"But I must. I mean to take the flyer going north. I shouldn't have missed one this morning."

THE CHILD LAY ASLEEP IN HER ARMS. — *Page 17.*

"There's no north-going flyer until after five o'clock. It's about a mile and a half to the station."

"I thought there was one at three."

"There is, but that goes east. It comes from Buffalo. That's why it's called the Buffalo flyer. You've time to cool off and escape the heat. The dinner's on. I was about to sit down when I heard your step. You'd better sit here. You'll not be so near the stove. I don't generally heat up this stove, but I was hungry for huckleberry pie, and the shanty stove doesn't bake well. It needs to be cleaned out."

She pushed a chair toward her visitor, who grew profuse in her thanks. Her voice was rich and full, with an accent unlike any which Debby Alden had ever heard. To her, all who did not speak English as she spoke it were foreigners. In this class she at once placed her stranger guest, whose mellow liquid tones were music in themselves.

"French," said Debby to herself. "I've

been told that they have such a soft, pretty
way of speaking."

Her guest was eating heartily. Debby
passed her the platter of meat. "Help
yourself," she said, with great open-hearted-
ness. "You'll have a walk before you, and
a long journey besides. You must eat if
you want strength to go on."

The woman reached forth her hand for
the dish. The act brought her long taper
fingers into prominence.

Debby Alden started. In the hand she
recognized the racial marks and standing
of the woman before her.

The prejudices and dislikes of generations of Aldens came to the front. Drawing herself up rigidly, she arose from the
table and let her guest finish her meal alone.

CHAPTER II

THE stranger finished her dinner in silence. She may have understood the thoughts which had flashed through the mind of her hostess. It was evident that she was used to such treatment as was accorded her here.

The child awakened, and she hurried to it, crying out: "Mammy's coming. Don't cry, honey."

Debby brought out a pitcher of morning's milk and cut a generous slice from the loaf of bread.

"You had better feed her now," she said. "Perhaps you had better take a bottle of milk with you if you have a long journey. The milk bought in cities isn't always as pure as it might be."

"It would be so much trouble — " began the woman; "and you are tired."

"What if I am? Being tired has harmed no one yet, as far as I know." She was already rinsing a small bottle and filling it. "I'll set it on the ice on the porch. You can get it when you are ready."

The child was devouring its bowl of bread and milk with a good healthy appetite. Debby could not but look at it. The child was beautiful, with soft, dark eyes fringed with long lashes, and soft, waving hair, which clung in rings to the white forehead.

The guests lingered until the heat of the midday had passed. Debby made ready a lunch for the child, and hastened them on their way.

"If you cross the tracks up there by the wagon road," she said, indicating the end of the yard, "you will have better walking, and it won't be so long."

"But the trains — " began the woman, timidly.

"There's no danger. There's no shifting

now, as you can see. They're only empty
box cars that are standing on the siding.
The regular trains come in about five o'clock,
and then there's freights all night long.
I've lived here all my life, and I've seen
precious little shifting this time in the day."

The woman took up the child and set out
for town. Debby Alden went with her to
the gate, and then turned to take in the
clothes on the line. A grocery wagon was
driving up with her supplies. She told the
man to put them on the kitchen table while
she gathered together the clothes and took
down the line.

The man did as he was requested, and then
turned his team toward town. Debby had
about finished her work, when she heard
the whistle of the east-bound flyer.

"I declare! I forgot all about that train,"
she said aloud. "But 'twon't be no difference. If she's any kind of a walker, she'll
be a considerable distance in town by this
time."

Despite her words, an uneasy feeling was with her. She walked to the front fence and looked up the road. The clothes-line was wound about her arm from thumb to elbow.

She saw the groceryman whip his horses and tear down the road at a reckless rate. The flyer had entered the yard, but, contrary to custom, was moving slowly back.

Quick as a flash Debby Alden grasped what had happened. She turned from the yard and ran down the hot, dusty road, regardless of heat and dirt. She came to the crossing almost as soon as the train reached there. The trainmen were bending over the body of the woman, which had been hurled against the slope of the mountain. She was past help.

"She's a stranger hereabouts," said some one. "I know every one that lives here, but I never saw her before. Where shall we take her?"

Here Debby Alden pushed to the front.

"Take her to my house," she said. "It's my fault that she's dead. I've killed her. Bring her along."

Some had a stretcher in readiness. Debby waited until all was ready, and then started to lead the way. She stopped suddenly and looked about her. "But the child! There was a child! Where is it?"

"She threw something from her just as the train struck," said the engineer. "I don't know what. I knew I couldn't stop, — we were going so fast, — so I shut my eyes. I didn't want to see the end."

The others were looking about for the child. They found her deep in the clump of elder bushes, where she had been thrown. She was quite unharmed, and was reaching out to clutch the clusters of bloom about her.

Debby Alden seized her from the trainman's arms and looked her over. "There's not a scratch on her! It was Providence that she lighted on the bushes."

With the child in her arms, she started homeward, and the men who had gathered about took up their burden and followed her.

"You'd better send Doctor Heins down, and the undertaker," she called to the groceryman, as he drove away.

When she entered her home, she deposited the baby on the couch and set about to assist the men. She brought out her best linen and cared for the dead woman as though she was near kin.

The baby cried, and she cared for it. The men went on about their own affairs, except two, who awaited the coming of the doctor. Debby kept busy from room to room, and all the while her mind was filled with thoughts of the peculiar position in which she was placed. She questioned how much of her knowledge would best be kept to herself, and how much it was right and proper for her to tell.

The doctor came, and, close at his heels,

— for the news of the accident had taken wings, — was Mrs. Bowerman with her baby in her arms, and the other women of the neighborhood, some curious and some actuated in their coming by a desire to be helpful.

They sat about in the kitchen and living-room. Debby herself went with the doctor into the parlor, where the woman lay. Each woman was curious and anxious, and wished to see the stranger. But Debby did not invite them to enter the front room, and they stood so in awe of her that they could not venture of their own accord.

Doctor Heins was a genial little Dutch-man, with shoulders hunched up, and blink-ing, near-sighted eyes. He examined the dead woman.

"I knew there was no use of your com-ing," said Debby. "She was quite dead when the men took her up. But the folks would be sure to say something if I hadn't sent for you."

"Yes, it's better to have a doctor here, though I'm really of no use. It's a case for the coroner. But I'll attend to that, Debby." He had caught her expression of perplexity. "I've done it before, and I'll see to it now. It isn't work for a woman."

He was bending over the dead woman, trying to discover in her features a likeness to some one he knew.

"She was certainly a fine-looking woman. Have you any idea who she was or where she was going?"

"She came from a distance, and she meant to go a long way off. That's all I know. I didn't ask her any questions, and she didn't tell me of her own accord."

Mechanically the doctor took the woman's hand in his own. It was the hand of one not accustomed to work. His near-sighted eyes blinked nervously as he examined it.

"This is unusual," he said. "She's been dead less than three hours, yet mortification has set in. The tops of her finger nails are quite purple."

He looked up at Debby, expecting her to reply. But she had moved to the end of the room, where she stood by the door as though waiting for him to leave.

"There comes Hallers, now; I hear the sound of wheels." She opened the door and passed into the living-room, and the doctor followed. She knew that her neighbors were waiting to hear her story. She did not wish to discuss it, but she thought it best to tell them enough to satisfy them. With this purpose in mind she passed into the kitchen and became the centre of the group gathered there. One woman arose and pushed her into a chair, saying, as she did so, "There, sit down! I should think you'd be all wrought up and of a tremble, Debby Alden!"

"Well, I'm not," she replied. "This all came so sudden that I haven't had time to be in a tremble. I've had no time to think of myself."

"They say that she stopped here," said a shrill-voiced little woman by the window. "Did you know her, Debby? Seeing that she was here and you took her in, I thought maybe you knew her."

"No, I didn't. She was walking toward the station." Then she repeated the incidents of the morning, omitting no detail. Her listeners sat breathless, drinking in each word of her story. There were exclamations of surprise, and sighs suggestive of their regret at the sad turn of affairs. Now and then Kate Bowerman's nervous, hysterical laugh rang over all; and the little child lay in the living-room and gurgled and laughed, unconscious of the tragedy close at hand.

"What kind of a woman did she appear to be? Did she look as though she might be some one?" It was Kate Bowerman who asked the question. Debby Alden knew what she meant. Throughout the valley the old residents rated family high. To

say that he belonged to "good stock" was
the highest compliment they ever paid to
any man.

Debby evaded a direct answer. "She
seemed able to pay her way and was well-
dressed. She was not a bad-looking woman.
I know you'll all say that when you come
to look at her."

"What sort of a spoken woman was
she?" asked the nervous shrill-voiced
woman sitting near the window. The
women were all talking at once, expressing
themselves as to the possible identity and
destination of the stranger, but the voice
of this one rose above all.

Debby Alden hesitated. She was one
who spoke the truth even to the merest
detail. She wondered at herself that she
now had a desire to keep something back.
It may have been that telling ill of the
dead restrained her.

"She was as nicely spoken a woman as
you'd want to hear, although she had an

odd way of saying her words. She must have come from far off, for no one about here talks any way like her."

"A foreigner, likely," said the shrill-voiced woman.

"Yes, she wasn't an American. I'm sure of that," said Debby.

"Do you think she might be German? There's a German settlement in the eastern part of the State. Did she talk anything like the help that Mrs. Stevenson had? Her girl Ricka was Dutch."

Debby shook her head. When she spoke, it was with her usual vehemence.

"Dutch! She talked no more like Ricka than I do. Her words were soft and full, and her voice was low. Mine sounded like bellowing alongside of it."

"French. They talk so," said Mrs. Bowerman. "They're not a bad-looking set as a whole, and they're neat. You said this woman looked trim and neat. Had she dark eyes and hair?"

"Very. Black. I've never seen blacker."

"Likely French." She arose, and, passing into the living-room, brought out the child. It went from the arms of one to another, who examined it critically until each detail of dress and feature was known.

The child's dress was sheer and fine and without adornment of any kind except the daintiest bits of handwork. It bore the marks of the best care and taste.

The little woman by the window held it close to her for an instant. "Poor child," she said, and her voice came down the scale until her words were scarcely audible. "You're laughing and cooing now, for you don't know what it means to lose a mother."

But her tenderness was swept before the clamor of the others' tongues.

The women lingered until called home by household duties. Several came back in the evening, bringing their husbands, and together they sat with Debby the long night through, it being considered a show of disrespect for any one to sleep in the house where the dead lay.

The third day after the accident, the woman was buried, and Debby Alden, who censured herself for advising the stranger to cross the tracks at the danger point, paid the funeral expenses, and saw to it that she was not laid in the plot reserved for the friendless dead. The question of caring for the child now came up. Debby was willing to give it a home until the relatives could be found. A notice of the accident with all the details was published far and wide.

But by Debby's holding back a little of her knowledge, a false coloring was given to these newspaper reports. They described the woman as French. The accounts left no doubt in the minds of the reader that the unfortunate stranger was the parent of the child. These reports were copied far and wide. More than one person to whom the child was dear, glanced at the head-lines and then read eagerly, only to toss the paper aside, having no vital interest in this French mother and her babe.

Several weeks passed, and the child was yet with Debby Alden. This additional care, with the housework, the cow and chickens, kept her busy. But the child had but one change of clothing, and she set to work to make others for it.

Such was her sense of duty that she selected for this little stranger the same material and style of garment that she would have done had the child been her own. She was awkward in the use of the needle. So she studied each detail of the little dress which the child wore, and copied it as closely as she was able. The rolled hems were beyond her comprehension, yet not beyond her conquering. When she found that she could not make the hems in the new dresses as they were in the old, she walked into town and called upon Miss Richards.

This Miss Richards was a spinster of middle age who had opened a free kindergarten for the mere love of the work, and who did needlework after the fashion of gentlewomen of generations passed. She was a refined, wholesome woman, who had spent her life among the beautiful things of the world.

She took up Debby's work. "A rolled hem is what you wish," she said. "It is easily done when once you know how to start it." She set Debby right, and Debby, who was neither dull nor lazy, carried the baby and work-bag home, where she sat up half the night until she had made a hem as smooth and fine as a cord.

She was not alone during these first weeks with the baby. The curious-minded of her neighbors came often to see her. Mrs. Bowerman was among these. She was a dozen years older than Debby Alden. She had married late in life, and had but one child, a puny little daughter, but a few months older than the little visitor at the Alden home.

Mrs. Bowerman was bitter toward all the world and critical of all that came within her range, except Mary, her own little child.

"Don't she walk yet?" she asked one day, as she watched the baby creep about. "Why, my Mary walked everywhere before she was as old, and she was into everything."

"An inheritance, perhaps," said Debby, grimly, "— her being into everything."

At every point Debby met her criticism with a touch of sarcastic wit. From early girlhood days, Kate Bowerman had tried to form her opinions and mark out her course of action; but Debby would have none of her. It was not that Kate's suggestions were not often most excellent, but, as Debby expressed herself, "It was not in the Aldens to be druv."

She had not thought of keeping the strange child as her own, until Kate Bowerman touched on the subject, when she ran across lots one afternoon to see how affairs at the Alden home were moving along.

"Doctor Heins was up at Barners' last evening. Grandmother Barner had another one of her spells, and I ran over to see if I could help Eliza out. When the old lady got easy, we fell to talking of this tramp's child. Doctor Heins said he knew you'd end in keeping it. But I sent him off with a bee in his bonnet. 'You don't know the Aldens,' I said. 'They're great hands for standing by their own flesh and blood, but when it comes to giving to an outsider, they're close. If some of the child's own folks don't turn up to claim her, you'll see her sent off to the poorhouse. You don't know the Aldens like I know them, root and branch.' That's what I told him."

While she was talking, Debby kept her needle busy on some little petticoats she was making. A nervous jerk showed as she took a stitch. Not until that moment did she make up her mind what to do with the child.

"It looks as though you didn't know them as well as you've counted on," she said. "You never heard tell of one of the Aldens turning a stranger from his door. Have you? I've never heard of them doing that, and I know their history for generations back. Debby Alden won't be the first to do such a thing. If her folks don't come to claim her, she'll stay here."

"But what will you call her? You can't have a child about the house without a name." Kate laughed maliciously.

"I'll call her Alden. It's a good name. There's never been no shame touched it. I'm the last of my folks, and I mean to give my name to this child. She'll have a good name. I defy any one to say a word against it."

Kate sank back in her chair. "Debby Alden! You've gone crazy. You're gone clean out of your head. You don't mean —"

"Yes, I do. I mean to call her Hester

Palmer Alden, after my own mother. I was always fond of the name Hester."

"But if her folks should come and take her after you've had her and grown fond of her! A baby does get on the soft side of a person, say what you will."

"I hain't going to trust to chance. I mean to make her mine by law. The Aldens never were slack about business. Not one of them even died without having his will drawn up and signed years before it was needed; and I don't intend to be the first to leave affairs to chance. I mean to go in to the county-seat and have the papers drawn up, so that there never can be any trouble."

She carried out her intentions before the week had gone. She took the unknown child before the court, and returned with it bearing the name of Hester Palmer Alden; but, with the Alden characteristic of keeping their affairs to themselves, she told no one except her legal adviser what she had done.

CHAPTER III

LITTLE HESTER thrived and grew after a new and remarkable way all her own, if Debby's statements could be taken as unbiassed ones. Never before in all the valley had a child lisped her first words as prettily as little Hester Alden; and never had another child had such sweet, attractive ways as she. She stole into Debby Alden's heart before the woman was aware, — for she had meant only to do her duty by the child, — and had filled it to the exclusion of all else.

Debby began to study the manner and dress of other children the age of Hester. She wished Hester to stand equal to any of them. Her spare moments were given to making dainty garments for the child. She had even subscribed for a magazine which made a specialty of child-life, and pored over its pages most assiduously.

Before Hester was three years old, she had accomplished some excellent results, for she had made of Aunt Debby an excellent needlewoman, and throughout the country-side had given her a reputation of being an authority on the proper care of a child. Aunt Debby, as Hester had been taught to call her, had fed, bathed, and trained the child according to the rules of the magazine. The results were all that could be desired. Hester was a dimpled, healthy, active child, as happy and contented as one could wish.

Debby Alden was uncertain regarding the age of the child. But feeling that to be without a birthday was quite as great an affliction as being without a name, she set aside the first day of June, and taught Hester to look upon it as the anniversary of her birth.

"The child must have a birthday," she explained to Miss Richards, who was the only person with whom she discussed her.

"I took the first of June because those days are generally warm and bright, and I mean her to have picnics and birthday cakes whenever she's old enough to understand."

Hester's fourth birthday was celebrated by a picnic in the orchard. Again had Debby gone by the book, inviting four little girls to spend the afternoon and having a cake with four pink candles burning on it.

Mary Bowerman was among the guests. The sight of the birthday cake with its tiny lights aroused in her little breast the same envious, malicious feelings which were the striking characteristics of her mother. The child was almost five years old, and had never had such a fuss made over her birthday as Hester was having. She sat down under the sweet apple tree, quite a distance from the others, refusing to take part in the festivities.

Debby was spreading the table, and called to her to come and play Ring-around-Rosy with the children. But she would not. Then Jane Orr, dimpled, pudgy, and beaming with good-will and good-humor, broke from the circle and ran to Mary to beg her to take part in the fun.

"You'd better come," she whispered, "or maybe Miss Debby will not let you come to the table. She's made ice cream. I saw the freezer hid under the berry bushes. You had better come, Mary. It's the nicest party I was ever at. I wish I was Hester Alden and could have a birthday cake with candles. Don't you? Aren't you glad she is having it?"

"I'm glad she has something, if it is only a party. But I'd rather have a father and mother. She hasn't either."

Her childish voice carried far. Little Hester heard, and for the instant was on the verge of tears. She had never thought of that before, yet it was quite true, she had neither father nor mother. She might have cried, had not Jane cried out, "Yes, but she has her Aunt Debby, and she's better than lots of fathers and mothers."

Hester smiled through her tears. She did have Aunt Debby. That was true. Perhaps if little girls have aunts, they're not supposed to have mothers, she reasoned, and for the time was satisfied with her conclusions.

Debby Alden caught the import of Mary's speech. She was not vexed with the child, for she saw that she did not understand the meaning of her own words. She had caught the idea from overhearing the speech of her elders at home.

Debby spoke to her sharply. "Come and play with the others, Mary Bowerman, and don't talk about things that a little girl can't understand." Then she turned about and whispered so that the others could not hear, "If I ever know of your speaking to Hester about having no father nor mother, I'll shake you until I break every bone in your body." Then she said aloud: "Now run and play with the others. Hester, let Mary have the handkerchief to drop. She's company."

For Mary's speech concerning Hester, Debby cared little. They were children. One could not expect much of babies five years old, yet Debby realized that this speech was a forerunner of many which Hester must meet either from the malicious-minded or from the thoughtless. She dreaded the time when Hester must be sent to school. Yet when she thought of these matters, she added grimly, "But there's one thing not one of them can ever tell her. I'm glad I kept a close tongue in my head the day the child's mother was buried."

She watched the child with jealous eye, fearful always that she would show some trace of her parentage.

"Blood's bound to tell," she would say to herself. "I know that's true, and I won't try to deceive myself by saying it hain't; but if there's anything in training,

I'll see to it that she's trained out of every
low trait that might have been born in her."

Miss Richards was her greatest help at
this time. She went to her for suggestions
whenever her own natural wit failed her.
The high-bred, cultivated woman was always
ready to help, and her suggestions were
ones that Debby Alden knew were worthy
of acceptance.

"Hester is over to Bowermans'," she
said one afternoon, as she came into Miss
Richards' living-room. "I've come to another place in the road where I don't know
which way to turn."

"And no sign-boards pointing anywhere,
Debby?" Miss Richards asked with a smile.

"Not a one. If there had been, I would
not have bothered you by coming."

"You never bother me. You know that,
Debby. I'm interested in Hester's welfare
almost as much as you are. I will not say
as much, for you hold a place in her life
that no one else can hold.

"I have just a little business to attend
to with one of the servants who is going
away for a visit. Excuse me until I speak
with her, and then we'll talk of Hester."
She left the room, leaving her caller alone
in an easy-chair by the window.

Debby looked about her, taking in each
detail of the apartment. Since Hester had
been with her, her eyes had grown keener.
She wished the child to have the best things
of life, and, to do Debby Alden justice, she
had the proper conception of what the
best things were. She wished her to be
honest and upright, and independent in
thought and action — Debby, in her own
heart, despising servility. These virtues
were the backbone of character. In addition to these, she wished Hester to be gentle
in manner, dainty in dress, and refined in
speech. And so she looked about her and
studied the environment which had made
Miss Richards what she was.

There were soft rich rugs, a few beautiful

pictures, the open piano with the sheet music upon the rack, a single rose in a plain little vase; an easy-chair or two, and the work-basket filled with exquisite handwork.

She had scarcely made a mental inventory of the room, when Miss Richards returned. Taking up her work, she sat down near her caller.

"Now, Debby, what about the roads? Where is it you wished to go?"

"I've been allowing Hester to play with Jane Orr. She's a nice-mannered little girl. Her mother trains her well, and I felt that Hester would learn something by playing with her."

"Yes, did she?"

"Yes, she did, and she's been troubling me ever since. You see, Miss Richards, Mrs. Orr tells Jane stories. I don't understand just what kind they are, for Hester gets them badly mixed up when she repeats them to me. But anyhow, they're the kind that children like. At least, Hester does, and she's pestered me ever since to have me tell her stories like Jane's mother tells."

"It would be all right, Debby. The very best educators of the day believe in telling children all manner of myths and fairy tales. I cannot see that it would do the child harm. Since she asks for them, I think I should tell her."

Debby smiled grimly. "That wasn't what troubled me. I believe in telling them to her. But when you never were told any yourself and don't know any, what's to be done?"

"That is easily remedied," was the reply. "I think I have what you need."

Selecting several volumes from the book shelf, she glanced hurriedly through them.

"This will do for a beginning," she said, handing the books to Debby. "Take them home with you. The stories are all short, and are generally pleasing to children.

Read them once or twice, and then tell
them to Hester. There's a lesson in each
little tale. The 'Necklace of Truth' is
good. It teaches a child to despise a lie."

"I'll see to it that she is taught that,"
was the grim response. "If I should ever
catch her in a lie, I believe I'd break every
bone in her body. Lying is such a low-down
trick."

Debby took the book home and read it
after Hester was in bed and asleep. It
was a collection of the old-time stories,
bits of myths and fairy tales which have
been told to the children for generations —
at least to most children. Debby Alden
herself had not been granted such a broad
culture. Her people had been rigid ad-
herents to the tenets of sect. The old
stories which Debby had heard in her childhood were awe-inspiring and terrifying.

She was soon master of the contents of
the book. She had kept her reading a
secret from Hester, and, when the child had

begged for a story, had put her off with promises for the future.

The mere reading of the stories had given her pleasure, for they opened a new world to her; a world filled with the rarest jewels of the imagination whose existence she had never suspected. But the pleasure which came to her from the reading was small compared to that which came to her when she took Hester in her arms, and, rocking slowly to and fro, repeated those wonderful tales to her.

Her first story, "The Necklace of Truth," Hester, big-eyed and eager, sat breathless until the story ended. Then giving a sigh of satisfaction, she said simply, "Tell it again."

The stories never grew old to the child. But when Debby's mind had fed upon them, she was hungry for more. Miss Richards was ready to satisfy her. More books were taken from the book-shelves to the Alden home. So it was that during

the winter of Hester's fifth year, Debby
revelled in myth and fairy tales, and bits
of quaint old classics, and fragments of
poem and rhyme.

Hester required much work and care
with her clothes, baths, and especially prepared meals, but Debby felt that she was
more than repaid for all her effort when
the child put her warm, chubby arms about
the woman's neck,'and in her pretty childish
prattle told of her love for Aunt Debby.

In the beginning of the sixth year, Hester
started to school. The district school, with
over half a hundred pupils of all grades
and ages packed in an ill-ventilated room,
was just at the end of the public road.
Debby had been reared in such an atmosphere, and realized its disadvantages. She
wished Hester to have greater opportunities than had been afforded her. The ward
building of the borough school was over
half a mile distant, and the many tracks of
the railroad lay between.

But when Debby Alden had a purpose clearly defined in her mind, she would admit no obstructions to its carryings. It was best for Hester to go to town; therefore it must be done, regardless of the cost to herself either physically or financially.

She walked with Hester each morning until she was safe beyond the dangerous crossing. At the close of each session she met her at the railroad. The walk home was neither long nor dull to them. Hester's tongue kept up a fire of talk about school, and Debby listened as one might listen to a sage. The subject never wearied her. She knew each evening what pupils had been publicly reprimanded, what color of waist and ribbon the teacher wore, and what lovely pictures the little girls had made with colored crayons.

"Miss Carns told us about Clytie and the sunflower yesterday," she began one evening, "and to-day she asked us children to tell her all about it."

"Could you?" asked Debby, eagerly.

"Yes; I knew that long ago. Miss Carns did not need to tell me. I always knew about Clytie turning into a sunflower. I could tell the story."

"And didn't you?"

"I was going to, Aunt Debby. Miss Carns said I might tell, and I got up. I was just telling it beautifully, and all the little girls sat still with their eyes 'bugging' out something terrible just to hear how much I knew, and then —"

She was almost in tears, and yet her indignation was enough greater than her humiliation that the tears were kept from falling.

"And what happened then? Did you forget? Tell Aunt Debby all about it." She held the child's hand closer in her own, as though to reassure her.

"No; I didn't forget. I never could forget about Clytie, Aunt Debby. Why, I have always known it. But Mary Bower-

man sat right back of me and punched me.
Yes, Aunt Debby," she nodded her head in
affirmation of her words.

"She punched me twice, and then I
turned and gave her a push, and —" the
lips quivered perceptibly, "and Miss Carns
said, 'Be seated, Hester!' She made me
sit down, and I couldn't finish about Clytie."

Debby Alden knew not what to say.
Her natural instincts were to sympathize
with the child, but her early training was
opposed to any such show of feeling as
tending to weakness and enervation.

"Well, I wouldn't cry about it. Miss
Carns may let you tell the story sometime
again. You may tell Mary that she's not
to punch you. You can tell her that before
you go into school to-morrow."

"I've told her already, Aunt Debby. I
waited until the line broke. She was at
the end, and I told her that if she punched
me that way again, I'd break every bone in
her body!"

Debby gave a gasp. The expression hurt her. The words were out of harmony with the child's beautiful countenance and manner.

"I don't believe that I would use such words, Hester. They do not sound nice."

"You use them, Aunt Debby." There was no criticism in the remark, only a mere statement of fact. "You wouldn't say anything that wasn't nice. Would you, auntie?"

Debby pressed her lips together. Her face took on its grim expression. She had used such words not once, but often. She had no wish to deny or palliate her offence. At last she spoke. "Yes, I have used those very words. I got into the habit of using them. No one ever told me they didn't sound well. I didn't know until I heard you say them. Then I knew. I will not use them again now, since I know how they sound, and I don't want you to say them either. Besides not sounding right, they're not truthful; for we both know that money couldn't buy us to break every bone in any one's body. We're simply telling a lie when we say we'll do it. Isn't that so, Hester?"

Hester pressed her lips prettily together and nodded her head in affirmation of Debby's words.

"Then let's not say it, auntie," she said seriously. "I don't want to be a liar."

But that expression, with many of its kind, had become the bone and marrow of Debby Alden's conversation. To cut this from her speech was like cutting into her flesh. But so long as a thing was right and proper, she would see to it that it was done, without regard to what it meant to her in effort and suffering.

Many times her tongue slipped over these expressions, but she remembered in time. "There! I've forgotten again, Hester," she would say grimly. "But I'm getting better.

It didn't come clear out that time. I stopped on the second word. I've gained something."

Debby's first heartache in connection with the child came at the close of the second month of school, when the report cards were sent home. The grades were marked in letters signifying excellent, good, medium, and poor. Debby examined the bit of pasteboard as a connoisseur would examine a work of art. She was wholly satisfied with the marks, for they were all G's.

But Kate Bowerman came over after supper to compare notes. It was then Debby's spirits fell, for Kate, after critically examining Hester's card, produced Mary's, on which E's marked every study.

Kate laughed maliciously, the laugh which in its mirthlessness sounded more like the cackle of a distracted hen. "I'd warm Mary soundly if she came home with a report that wasn't all Excellents," she said. "She knows that, and she gets her lessons before she gets her meals."

"She looks it," said Debby, pertinently, glancing from the thin, nervous, sickly child to where Hester, happy and hearty, stood.

CHAPTER IV

THE following morning Debby proved herself faithful to the family reputation of not being "slack." She not only saw that Hester was safe beyond the tracks, but she accompanied her into town and into the schoolroom.

Miss Carns came to the schoolroom door to meet her. "What has happened, Debby?" she cried, in her bright, airy little manner. "I haven't seen you for years, and now you have actually come to see me. Sit here by my desk. You can have a view of the children and all that goes on in the room."

She drew forward a chair for her guest. Debby sat down without a word. She felt out of place, and out of sorts with the world and all about her. For a dozen years she had been asleep to all that was going on

61

about her. Now, as her eyes slowly opened, she found wonderful changes, and she felt old and disinterested and out of harmony.

She looked at Miss Carns earnestly for a few moments. Then she spoke. "Do you know, Mabel, that I haven't seen or talked with you for over ten years?"

"Is it possible! You are right about it being so long. I remember now. We were on a sleigh-ride and took supper at Hammersley's old farm-house. I remember you and Jim Baker drove down in a cutter. My, what good times they were!"

Her face was all smiles and dimples as she spoke.

"Over ten years ago," said Debby, slowly, letting her glance move from head to foot of her companion, taking in each detail of her dress and manner. "And you don't look one day older."

"I'm not. I never intend to get old. It's out of fashion, Debby. As time goes, and if I live, I suppose I'll have a seventieth birthday. But I'll be seventy years young, Debby, not seventy years old. I really never mean to be over twenty in spirits. I may not be able to keep the wrinkles from my face, but I shall keep them from my heart." She laughed again. The children looked up at her with a smile. No wonder they loved Miss Carns. Life was so happy and sweet with her, and she reflected her own mind upon theirs.

But her words depressed Debby Alden. There were many phases of life in which she was yet a child. For the first time she was thoroughly dissatisfied. She had kept herself in the old home, living the life of a recluse and resting upon the old honors of the Alden family, while opportunities and youth had slipped from her. She studied the woman before her, and smiled grimly. She knew Mabel Carns's age to the day — just six months older than Debby Alden herself; but looking ten years younger, and as bright and happy in manner and heart as a care-free child.

"No; you don't look a day older than you did when we drove down to Hammersley's farm."

"That's nice. Did you walk into town to tell me that, Debby?"

Her words recalled Debby to the purpose of her visit. "No, I didn't. I came to see about Hester. I'm not satisfied."

"Not satisfied! What has happened? She is a lovely child in school and as bright as the average child. I know no reason for your being dissatisfied."

"She got only G's on her report."

"But, Debby, that is good. A great many did not receive G. If I were you, I would be quite satisfied with such a report."

"But there were reports marked Excellent in everything."

"Yes; one or two. But the children who received those were unusual pupils

— or above the average age; or," and at that instant her glance fell upon Mary Bowerman, sitting at her desk with her shoulders hunched up and her eyes fixed upon an open book, "or they study out of school."

"Hester can do that. I'll see to it that she does."

"But I do not approve of a child of six years working at lessons at home. What they do in school will be enough. It will be better that they grow strong and healthy."

"I have no intention of overworking Hester. She's as strong as a piece of hickory. I'll not let her overdo."

Miss Carns gave a sigh, and yielded to the stronger will. "Well, if you are quite determined, Debby, I presume you must have your own way. I'll give her a reader to carry home, and I'll mark out the lesson."

"But I wanted more. I've heard Hester

tell about the reading. You do things different from when you and I learned to read. I don't quite understand."

"Simple as can be. Stay this morning, and you'll see how children are taught by new methods."

Debby sat half the morning watching Miss Carns go through the work with a skill and despatch which was marvellous to one ignorant of the newer methods.

When she was ready to go, Miss Carns gave her several books on the subject, and she went from the schoolroom with arms laden with texts on the word and sentence method.

At the corner of Erie Avenue and Fifth Street she met Kate Bowerman and Mrs. Mullin on a shopping expedition.

"You'd better come along, Debby. There's a new department store opened up in the Leonard Block. This is their opening day, and they're serving coffee to all the women that come in." Kate laughed. Her voice clung on its high falsetto note as she added, "Come and get a decent cup of coffee once in your life."

"Come along," urged Mrs. Mullin. "I've heard that they have fine goods. We might as well go and see. It doesn't cost anything."

Debby turned and went with them. She was so ignorant of the business interests of the town that she had heard nothing of the proposed changes. As they walked down the Avenue, she turned to her companion with the question: "Who's starting the store? What kind of a one is it — general?"

"Every kind, but arranged differently from what a general store is. Each kind of goods has its own room, but they all open into each other; and they have some of the store on the second floor."

"Oh!" said Debby. "Who did you say was going to keep it?"

"No one from hereabouts. A man by

the name of Stout. Ab, I think, is his first name. Short, I suppose, for Abner. My! don't it look fine? And to look at the folks going in!"

They had come directly in front of the store whose windows were gaudy with all manner of finery for house and person. A steady flow of shoppers was pouring in through the open door. The three women crossed the street and joined the crowds of visitors. At the rear of the grocery department, a young girl was serving coffee and wafers to the women, and all the while delivering a harangue upon the particular brand of berry they had for sale.

She was a pretty girl with dark curly hair, sharp dark eyes, and a business-like manner.

"Who is she?" asked Debby, between her sips of coffee.

"Ab Stout's daughter. They say he has six girls. His wife is dead," whispered Mrs. Mullin, bending close that the subject of the conversation might not catch her words.

"Indeed. She's inclined to be pretty," said Debby. "Indeed, I might say she'd be beautiful if it wasn't for her sharp features. I never like sharp features."

At this Kate Bowerman leaned over and whispered: "My! but don't she resemble your Hester! Take a good look at her, Debby. They're alike enough to be sisters."

Debby did look. The soft hair with its waves and the great dark eyes of the two were not unlike, but the features and expression were wholly different.

They had finished their coffee and were moving toward another department, when Kate began: "I never before saw so great a resemblance as Hester has to that girl. If they were the same age, they'd be enough alike to be twins." She stopped and looked directly at Debby. "Suppose it should

chance that Hester belonged to this Ab
Stout. Now, when I come to think of it,
I remember Sam speaking about Stout,
saying his wife and little girl died the
same time. Do you suppose —"

If her purpose was to discomfort Debby,
she was disappointed, for Debby looked her
straight in the eye and said unconcernedly:
"No; I don't suppose. I know there isn't a
drop of their blood in Hester's body."

"You can't be sure of that unless you
know her people, and you —"

"I know that much," said Debby.
"There's no use of talking any more
about those people."

Her words set Kate Bowerman to thinking. Kate knew that Debby spoke the
truth at all times, and in all its harshness.
It was not to be doubted, then, that she
knew something of her foster-child's parentage.

It is natural for one to attribute to others motives similar to those which have a

place in one's own mind. Kate Bowerman was self-centred and selfish. Her mind
had never been able to conceive the reason
for Debby Alden's taking into her home
and caring for a strange child. But now
Debby's words opened her mind's eye to
possible reasons. Debby knew more of
the child's people than she had ever let
others know. Were they people of
wealth and importance, to whom Debby
would later make known the identity of
the child, with the hope that they would
amply repay her for her trouble? Kate's
thoughts ran in that direction, although
she was not able to reach a conclusion.

Debby let all thought of the Stout family
pass from her mind. The evening of that
same day she read through the teacher's
manual on the methods of teaching and
reading to the little folk. The suggestions
were concise, and without any professional
terms. This, with what she had seen in
school that day, made the subject clear

to her. She saw what the educator had in mind. Her own common sense helped her to know that his ideas were sound. She was in sympathy with him from the first, and took up his system with the enthusiasm of a young teacher. Love could not give her skill, but it could and did give her patience and ambition.

Each evening she labored long with Hester, reviewing the lessons of several days past, and teaching her the new words which came in the lesson for the following day. After the Christmas holidays, Hester brought home a memory gem, a little poem of child life which all the children in school were to commit to memory.

Debby read the selection, for Hester had handed it to her the moment they had entered the house from school.

"I like that, Hester. It is beautiful. I declare, I felt like crying while I read it. The moment the supper work is cleared away, we'll study it."

The reading was too difficult for a little six-year-old. Debby read it aloud, line by line, and Hester repeated it after her. The entire evening passed before a stanza had been committed, the woman finding that her memory, from disuse, was almost as weak as the child's.

So the winter passed, with days spent in school and evenings in study. Hester was not quick to grasp the lessons, but when once learned, they remained with her. For this reason her report cards during the spring term, when Miss Carns spent much of the time in oral review, improved perceptibly. Several poems had been learned during the year. Hester was able to repeat all, standing very erect and prim, and making quaint little bows and gestures, as her Aunt Debby had taught her.

The last week in May marked the close of school. The little folks gave an entertainment on the afternoon of the last day.

Debby went early in order not to miss any of the programme. She wore a stiff black silk dress, one which had done service since her twentieth birthday. The black, shining surface and severe lines intensified the angles of her form and face, making her look years older than she was. She sat up primly in her stiff-backed chair, her hands folded upon her lap.

The room soon filled with visitors. There was a rustle of silken petticoats and the delicate subtle fragrance of choice perfumes. Young matrons, whose first babies had but entered school, and silver-haired grandmothers sat eager and anxious to hear that one in whom they were most interested.

Debby Alden looked about her and studied the faces and attire of these people, most of whom she had known in her school days. Again the old dissatisfied feeling came to her. She seemed older —years older than the grandmothers. The

world was all disjointed, and nothing fitted
in.

Her heart beat high when Hester came
forward, and with quaint bow and gesture said her little speech. Her effort was
neither better nor worse than that of the
other children, but to Debby's infatuated
eyes, it was far finer than any other. For
a moment her elation at Hester's success
caused her to forget herself and those
about her; but only for a moment, for
the child came up to her, and, leaning against
her, had whispered: "Look at Jane Orr's
mother. Isn't she sweet, Aunt Debby?"

Debby looked and saw a plain little
woman, beautified by a wonderful smile,
and dainty and sweet in a soft white gown,
and a soft haze of hair about her forehead.
Then Debby realized the cause of her
dissatisfaction. Hester was old enough to
notice the difference in women. She was
heart-sick with fear lest the child should
find her plain and unattractive. She

knew not what to do. Then she thought of Miss Richards. She would go to her.

When the entertainment was over, she sent Hester home with Jane Orr, and she went to call on Miss Richards. Without preliminary talk, she opened her heart to Miss Richards, telling her what she dreaded.

"Hester is all I have," she said simply. "I think I should die if she'd take to comparing me to other folks and find me dull and old-fashioned. That's what I dread."

"Yes, I understand, Debby. But you are not naturally dull, and you are not old. A woman of thirty has just begun to live. To my mind, she has but reached the place where she has judgment enough to know what living means. I repeat, Debby, that you are not naturally dull. Take my advice, and don't allow yourself to become so."

"But what can I do to help myself?" she asked. "I'm alone the greater part

of the day. Down our way women don't
visit when they are my age. There's a
set of young girls of eighteen who go about
some, but, for the most part, they settle
down at home when once they marry.
I'm afraid they'd look upon me as peculiar if I'd dress up in white and fluff my
hair."

Miss Richards realized that this was
no light subject of conversation. Although
it dwelt on gowns and hair-dressing, beneath was the question of a woman's happiness and peace of mind. To Miss Richards there was a trace of the tragical in it.
After a moment's deliberation, she replied: "Debby Alden, haven't you yet
learned to do what is right and proper
without caring what might be thought of
it? If you mean to be influenced by the
opinions of others, you will change your
mind every hour of the day. Before we
go further, let me tell you how I was reared,
Debby. I'm twice your years, and yet

I wear white gowns, and sometimes I put a flower in my hair."

Laying aside her needlework, she crossed the room and sat close beside her guest. She told of that broader life in distant towns, where years brought to a woman greater capabilities and a wider, freer range of vision; where age broadened in place of narrowed one's power for enjoyment. She described the ways of women whom she remembered when she herself was a young girl. When she had finished her story, Debby Alden was convinced of two things: the first, that she had let many a golden opportunity slip from her; the second, that from that time on she would follow out her own inclination, without repression and without regard to what others might say.

During the summer, encouraged by Miss Richards, she grew blooming and radiant. She did as she would have done had not the tendency of the valley been

set against it. She dressed herself in becoming dainty dresses. She opened the
old piano and brought back to memory
the few old tunes she had learned at singing school. Hester, big-eyed and wondering, could not understand the cause of
this transformation. But she was pleased
beyond words to express. One evening as
she stood by the piano, her childish voice
at intervals catching the air and carrying
it along, she stopped suddenly, and, throwing her arms about the woman's neck,
cried out, "Aunt Debby, you are perfectly
beautiful!"

It was in this atmosphere, this struggle
after a broader, fuller culture, that Hester
Alden spent her childhood. She was in
ignorance of the mystery concerning her
identity. She knew only that her mother
had been killed at the railroad crossing,
and that Debby had taken her, then a
baby, to live at the Alden home. She
had taken it for granted that her mother

and Debby Alden were sisters, for she
had heard her aunt frequently say that
her brothers had died in infancy. So her
life passed without any unusual occurrence
until she entered upon her first year at
the high school.

"Aunt Debby, you are perfectly beautiful!" — *Page 79.*

CHAPTER V

HESTER was but one of several hundred pupils in the high school. Several who had entered the primary grade at the same time were with her now.

Jane Orr, Mary Bowerman, Minnie Watson, and Orpha Sheddy were among these. The girls had studied together in school, and had walked to and from home arm in arm. Through Aunt Debby's efforts, Hester had been among the first in her class. Her standing had never been the result of unusual capacity for study or keenness of perception. Debby Alden had never failed to go over, day after day, each lesson, and with wonderful patience explain and illustrate the points which Hester was slow to grasp.

At the beginning of Hester's freshman

year, the principalship of the high school
changed. Mr. Lewis with his old-fashioned, conservative ideas was asked to
step aside, that a bustling, up-to-date man
with new ideas and new methods might
take his place. The new man was Professor Sanderson, who had fought his way
from backwoods school through college
and into the lucrative position of head-
master at R. Success to him meant nothing more than the capacity to earn money.
In his mind that man was most successful whose income was greatest. He had
no standard of success along ethical lines.
He himself was upright and honest, because it paid to be so. He was a stocky,
heavy-set man, with a round, bullet-shaped
head set closely on square shoulders. He
had a keen mind, bright, sharp eyes, and
sufficient energy and ambition to accomplish anything toward which his wishes
tended.

He introduced new methods in regard

to recitation and discipline. Some of his
ideas were an improvement upon the old
way, but by far a greater number robbed
a pupil of personal responsibility and put
them on the same moral footing as felons.
His ideas seemed to be that all young
people are naturally evil, and but wait an
opportunity to allow their tendencies full
sway. So he hedged them about by rules,
and punished to the extreme the slightest infringement of any of his iron-clad
laws. He knew no distinction between
a pupil who whispered and one who was
ready with a lie to clear himself.

It was near the end of the first month
of school. Hester, with her books strapped
together and her lunch basket in hand,
had crossed the tracks and was making
her way up Erie Avenue, when Mary and
Jane met her.

"Did you get out your Latin last
night?" asked Mary. She had not improved in looks since her primary days.

She was thin and sallow. Her movements were quick and nervous. She had inherited her mother's disposition so far as not wishing to be second.

"Yes, I can read every word of it."

"Did you do the translating yourself?" asked Mary, suspiciously. She had not been able to translate one sentence.

"No, not altogether. Aunt Debby and I worked together. She really read them first." Hester knew no reason for not making this statement. She felt pleased when she made a creditable examination, but her desires did not run toward outdoing her friends.

Jane smiled blandly. There was something whole-souled and attractive in her smile. She was a large girl, with a placid, sunny disposition. "I worked all evening at my Latin," she said slowly. "I thought I had it just right. I had each sentence written down beautifully, when Ralphie came in and read them over. He shrieked with laughter while he read, and then he carried the paper in to father and they laughed together."

"What was wrong?" asked Hester.

"Nothing much. I'd made a mistake in that fifth sentence, *Cæsar bonas leges habuit*." She said the words slowly as she made an effort to recall them. She smiled then, and continued: "Miss Watson is always telling us to catch at the meaning as far as we are able. I tried to please, and translated at sight."

"What did you make of it?" Mary asked the question eagerly. She had read the sentence without difficulty. She always found delight in doing that which her friends had found difficult. Now, without giving Jane time to reply, she repeated glibly, "*Cæsar leges bonas habuit*, 'Cæsar had good laws.' I can't see anything hard about that."

"But I translated by sound," said Jane, pensively. "I had it written on my paper,

'Cæsar has bony legs.' That was what made Ralph laugh so."

"I have that right," said Hester. "Indeed, I believe mine are all right. Aunt Debby is very particular. We look up every word."

"Can your Aunt Debby read Latin?" asked Jane in surprise. "That must make it nice for you — to have some one in the house that knows all about it."

"But Aunt Debby doesn't know all about it. She began to study when I did, and we go over the work together every evening. That is why I have been able to translate my sentences."

"Having to-day's lesson won't do you much good now," said Mary, eagerly. There was a suggestion of spite in her voice. "I'm glad I did not pore over my books last night. We'll have no recitation to-day. We're going to be examined. Written examination."

"Examinations!" Hester Alden gasped

for breath. The word sounded horrible
to her. It was almost as awe-inspiring as
though Mary had said, "To-day we go to
the guillotine."

Mary laughed. Her laugh was a faint
suggestion of her mother's.

"Yes, written. There'll be fifteen questions. They're to be difficult ones. The
whole two months' work is to be covered
by it. We may be kept at it all day."

"How do you know?" asked Hester.

"Oh, I know," laughed Mary. "But
I'm not telling."

"But I am," said Jane. She turned
toward Hester. "Mary and I were waiting in the outside office last evening. Professor Sanderson was in the private office
talking with Miss Watson. He told her
to make out fifteen questions to cover two
months' work, and to have them ready for
this morning. He said he wished the examination to be good and stiff." Jane
smiled blandly as she repeated the word.

To her the subject had its touch of humor.

"Miss Watson was angry. She did not hesitate to tell Professor Sanderson what she thought."

"She wasn't so very angry," said Jane. "She told him that she did not think it fair to her to give her so little time; that she had an engagement for the evening, and making out the questions would keep her up half the night."

"He could have had the examination some other day — either Thursday or Friday. This is only Wednesday," said Hester, who had gathered from her Aunt Debby some practical ideas.

"She said just that," cried Mary, "and what do you think he said? That he did not wish her to have longer than over night, for then she would have an opportunity to drill her class in the very questions she meant to ask."

"Did he say that?" cried Hester, angry

at the insult offered to this teacher whom
she greatly admired. "If I were Miss Watson, I would have —" She hesitated for
a word to express herself. She could
think of nothing quite adequate to the
occasion. Her old childish expression
flashed through her mind, but she did not
put it into words, for she and Aunt Debby
had passed beyond that place where they
declared themselves ready "to break every
bone in one's body."

"Let us walk faster," said Jane. "If
we go into school the moment the doors
are opened, we'll have time to do a little
reviewing. I really must glance over the
verb. I positively know nothing at all
about it."

"Don't tell the other girls," cried Mary,
"or they'll go in and review, too."

"Let them," said Jane. "I don't know
any reason why they shouldn't."

"They'll make better marks in their examination," she said.

Hester turned to look squarely at her. She had beautiful eyes, which seemed to have the power of looking deep into the innermost secrets of one's heart. Mary tried to meet Hester's glance, but her face flushed, and she turned aside.

"Suppose it does make their marks better," she said slowly. "That's why we'd tell them, so they could look over their work if they wished to." She paused just an instant, and then said quickly: "Do you know you're a dreadfully selfish girl, Mary Bowerman? You are always looking out for number one, and trying to get ahead."

It was not a kind remark; but it at least was a truthful one. Hester spoke without regard to consequences, and in this lay her fault. She was quick to express herself. Although her criticism was just and frank, it was none the less criticism, and cut its object to the quick.

Mary was not slow to take offence.

Quick as a flash an angry retort was upon her lips, when Jane interposed.

"Storms in a tea-cup," she said so blandly that both her companions smiled. "If Hester would not say all she thought, and Mary would not bubble over at the least jostle, what a happy time we could have!"

There was no resisting Jane's calm good-humor. She gave the girls no opportunity of replying, but took the conversation in her own hands for the time.

"There's Orpha. She must know about it."

Jane raised her voice to claim the girl's attention. Hearing her name called, Orpha looked back, and, seeing her friends, waited until they came up to her.

"We must tell her," Jane repeated.

"Much good it will do," said Mary. "If she had from now until commencement to study, she wouldn't know the difference between an adjective and a noun."

"Hush," said Jane, for they were now within speaking distance. She turned to Orpha and told her about the examination and how they had heard of it before the others. Orpha listened without a word. She was a dull girl with stolid, heavy features. She went about with several different sets in the high school, but was not a close friend with any particular girl. She was easy to get along with, for she never became excited, was never angry, was never known to be in a hurry; and, so far, had never been heard to express her opinion upon any subject or any person.

"We three are going into school the instant the door opens," said Hester. "Come along, Orpha, and we'll all study until school calls."

"What's the use?" said Orpha, stolidly. The expression of her face had not changed in the slightest. Nevertheless, she went with the girls into the building. They met a number on their way to whom they communicated the news of the examination, so that fully a score went into the assembly-room and fell upon the Latin text-book, tooth and nail.

Miss Watson was in the assembly-room in conversation with the teacher in charge. It was evident from her expression of face and nervous manner that she was greatly disturbed. A half-hour later, when the freshmen entered her class room, she was quite herself. She smiled grimly as she arose, and, standing by the desk with a paper in her hand, addressed the pupils. "Professor Sanderson has given me a diagram of the room, with the name of each pupil written upon the desk where he wishes him to sit. That will necessitate your being moved from your accustomed places. You understand the reason for my asking you to change. I'm acting under orders from a superior officer."

By this time the greater number of pupils had heard of the encounter between Miss

Watson and Professor Sanderson the previous evening. They appreciated the situation in which she was placed. She was a popular teacher; being herself a person of refinement and culture, she accorded to her pupils the utmost courtesy and respect. As a class, they were in sympathy with her.

With great despatch she located each pupil, saw to it that the material and questions for the examination were passed, and then resumed her place at the front of the room.

"You understand, of course, that there must be no help given. It is a test of your knowledge of the subject, and not of your neighbor's."

There was a movement of pens. For several hours not a sound except that or the movement of a pupil in order to rest his hand was heard. Miss Watson arose and walked about the room. Time dragged upon her hands. The noon hour passed, yet the brightest pupils had not completed the test.

"When you complete the work, lay the papers on my desk and go home," she said. She was taking this dismissal upon her own shoulders. Professor Sanderson had not given her authority to send them home until the close of the afternoon session. But Miss Watson had judgment enough to know that three hours of uninterrupted writing was too much of a task on the nerves of growing boys and girls.

There were fifteen questions. Hester had reached the thirteenth when a wad of paper came flying through the air and landed plump upon her desk. She looked up quickly in time to catch Mary Bowerman's nod and glance, signifying that the note was from her.

"What's the imperative of *sum*? Write it for me, and I'll let you have the fifteenth. It's hard."

Hester surreptitiously tore off a narrow

edge of paper, hastily scribbled thereon the desired information, and sent it flying back. A few minutes later, for Mary was delayed in her answering by Miss Watson's keen eyes fixed upon her, a return note with the answer to the fifteenth upon it, landed upon Hester's desk.

She was copying it when Professor Sanderson came into the room to speak to Miss Watson. She listened to what he had to say, nodded in reply, and then, turning to her pupils, said, "Before handing in your papers, write upon the upper margin of the first page whether you have or have not received or given help."

Hester finished her work, turned to her first page, and wrote across the top, "I have both given and received help." She was not a speedy worker at any time, and to-day the new experience of undergoing a written examination made her unusually slow. As she gathered up her papers and began to put them in order, she looked about the room. The class, with the exception of herself and two boys in a distant part of the room, had finished. Professor Sanderson was standing at Miss Watson's desk looking over the papers as they were handed in.

As Hester took her papers to the front of the room, the boys advanced with her, and the three papers lay side by side on the desk.

At this, Mary, Jane, and Orpha, who had been waiting in the cloak-room, came in. "We wish to speak to Miss Watson," they said to Hester. "Wait, and we'll walk down with you."

"Not so fast, young ladies," cried Mr. Sanderson, as he fixed his eagle eyes upon them. He held Hester's paper in his hand, upon which he had pounced as a cat upon a mouse. "Hah! hah! what have we here?" He held the paper before him, while he read slowly, "I have both given and received help." Then, turning to Hester, he asked sternly if that statement were true.

"Why, certainly, or why should I have written it?" she replied. She had never been cowed or browbeaten in her life. She had been taught obedience through love and reason. She wished to do the right thing because it was right. She had never been taught what fear meant. Now, quite unawed, she faced Professor Sanderson and answered him as freely as she would have answered Aunt Debby.

"Don't be pert, young lady. Remember to whom you are speaking, or you shall be taught to remember. There's a strange discrepancy here." He turned to address this last statement to Miss Watson. "This," tapping the paper with the edge of the glasses which he had just removed from his nose, "is the only paper which bears such a statement. As you see, there must be two parties to the transaction."

"It is very evident," said Miss Watson.

She made no pretence of being in sympathy with his method of conducting examinations.

He turned to Hester, and with his most impressive air, said, "And so you have the effrontery to stand up before me and declare that you have been dishonest?"

"Indeed, I have been nothing of the sort," she said with decision. "On the contrary, I have honestly said that I received help."

"Be careful, be careful. You must remember, young lady, to whom you are speaking. Your offence in being dishonest is quite enough, without adding impertinence. I demand respect from my pupils."

"It might be well to pay respect to them," said Hester. She was not afraid of Professor Sanderson, but she was trembling with anger. His sharp speeches were uncalled for and undeserved. She had no intention of bearing them as though they were due her.

Her three companions sank down upon the recitation bench nearest to them. Orpha looked as stolid and as disinterested as though Professor Sanderson had been passing remarks about the weather. Jane sat quiet, looking straight before her. She was thinking quickly during the few minutes.

Mary Bowerman moved restlessly. Her hands were not quiet for a moment. She fussed with her belt and her rings, while her glance moved quickly from one point to another.

Professor Sanderson squared his shoulders, pressed his lips together, and looking the undaunted Hester straight in the eye, said sternly, "To whom did you give help?"

"I cannot tell you."

"You *can* not tell me." He repeated the words slowly and impressively. "Do you mean to say that you have not the power of telling me, or do you mean to say that you *will* not tell?"

"I *will* not tell." Her anger had passed.
She was herself again. Her one thought
now was that she had better hurry home,
lest Aunt Debby would be waiting the
evening meal for her. Her voice was quite
calm, but decisive.

Professor Sanderson looked her directly
in the eye as though by force of will he
would compel her submission. She met
his gaze unmoved and fearless.

It was to be regretted that Debby Alden
did not see her then. Had she done so, all
fearful thoughts of the child's parentage
would have left her. For the blood of a
serf could not be in the veins of one who
defies the authority that would compel
him to do that which his sense of honor
could not sanction.

CHAPTER VI

DEBBY ALDEN had prepared supper, and sat down to wait Hester's coming. The old-fashioned drop-leaf table was set in the dining room. This was an innovation from the first of Hester's school days. It was not the only one. There were napkins upon the table and a bouquet of asters — the very last of the fall flowers. Debby had laid the table after the fashion laid down in a periodical devoted to questions of the home. It was dainty and attractive, without going beyond practical common sense.

Before the coming of Hester, Debby Alden had eaten in the kitchen, and had not used napkins, in order to save the washing. When there was need of such an article, she used the bottom of her kitchen apron. But Hester was younger, and must become accustomed to the use of napkins, or she would appear at a disadvantage when she was older and had formed the habits.

Debby waited until the hour at which Hester was in the habit of returning had passed. Then she grew uneasy. She looked from the window to see if the girl had come into the yard, and when she had not, she went to the gate where she could get a view of the road and crossing.

"She has gone somewhere with the girls," she said again and again to encourage herself. But when almost an hour had passed and Hester had not come, Debby put on her hat and started forth. She was never without an uneasy feeling about the railroad crossing. She stopped a moment at Mrs. Bowerman's to inquire if Hester were there. Learning that Mary had not come home, Debby's heart grew lighter. Nevertheless, she went on into town. As she came to Seventh Street and Ontario Avenue, the lights were turned on in the high school building. The lower floors were in darkness, but the third floor was fairly ablaze.

She made her way through the dark entrance and hallways, mounted the steep stairs, and came to the door of Miss Watson's recitation-room. The scene within caused her to pause. Miss Watson sat with weary head bowed upon her upturned palms. In the distant, shadowy part of the room, huddled together as though affected by fear, sat Jane, Mary, and Orpha. Hester stood at a front desk. Her hands were back of her, supported on the top of a desk. Her head was tilted back as she looked Professor Sanderson squarely in the face. Her dark hair hung in a single heavy braid down her back. Her cheeks were flushed and her eyes brilliant with feeling.

Debby Alden caught her breath and

stood. The persons within the room neither saw nor heard her.

"I have given you a half-hour to consider this matter, Miss Alden," Professor Sanderson was saying. He stood before her with his watch in his hand as though he had been timing her. He looked at her as though to compel her to do as he had asked.

"What have you to say now? Are you ready to tell me the name of the person who was a party to your dishonesty?"

"I deny that I was dishonest. I received and gave help. I have not denied it."

"Answer my question, Miss Alden. Give me the name of that person."

"I will not."

"Very well. I am accustomed to being obeyed. I have never yet allowed a pupil to transgress my laws or infringe upon the discipline of the rooms, nor do I intend to. You may remain in the room until you are ready to obey my commands."

"I will not tell either now or an hour later."

"The matter is settled. You remain here until you do, whether it be one hour or twenty-four."

He was about to pass into the adjoining recitation-room when Miss Watson spoke to him. She had arisen. Her usually pale cheeks were marked by a spot of crimson. Her dark eyes were brilliant with indignation, yet when she addressed him, it was with the courtesy and respect due to his position. "Professor Sanderson, will you not reconsider your words? I think you have spoken hastily."

"Hastily! I am not in the habit of speaking hastily, Miss Watson. I most assuredly shall not reconsider. You are out of your jurisdiction, Miss Watson. Your work is to attend to the work in Latin. I shall manage the discipline."

"Perhaps the matter is out of my juris-diction," she said quietly, "but this evening I mean to make it mine. I think Miss Alden is quite right in the stand she has taken."

Professor Sanderson had been standing at the door of the recitation-room. But at such revolutionary words he turned and came back into the room. He had not learned self-control, for he was trembling with rage. But Miss Watson, actuated in her words by a sense of justice, was not at all awed by his sputtering and show of anger.

"What! Is it possible, Miss Watson, that you have the audacity to stand there before my face and tell me that you take sides with a pupil against a principal? Is it possible? I shall see to it that my teachers as well as the pupils are disciplined. You have need of it."

"We'll discuss that later. At present the subject is Miss Alden. I surely do take sides with her. I must ask you to allow her to go home now. She has already been detained several hours."

"Never, until she is willing to do as I have commanded."

"Then I shall take the responsibility. Hester," turning to the girl who stood silent before her, "take your wraps and go home. You have been kept here long enough."

"You shall answer to me for this, Miss Watson," cried the principal. His face was crimson with rage. He had so lost his self-control that his voice rolled forth like a clap of thunder.

"I shall answer to the board of directors and the city superintendent," replied Miss Watson, quietly. "Go home now, Hester; your Aunt Debby will be alarmed about you."

"I'll stay, Miss Watson!" she cried, clinging to this teacher whom the pupils loved and admired. "My going home will cause trouble for you. I'll stay rather than that."

"Nonsense, child. There'll be no trouble

further than telling my story to the directors. Go, now." At this Debby Alden came into the room. That part of the conversation which she had overheard had left her all at sea as to the cause of offence or the remedy for it. Mr. Sanderson had already left the room, and knew not that she had entered. She came up to where Miss Watson and Hester stood. "What's the trouble?" she asked. "You haven't been misbehaving, Hester?"

"I don't know, Aunt Debby. You may think so."

"Sit down, Miss Alden," said Miss Watson, drawing a chair closer. "Let me tell you the story from the first. You can judge for yourself."

Debby Alden seated herself. Miss Watson repeated the events of the day. As far as possible, she kept her own opinions in the background.

"Hester received help on the fifteenth problem, and gave help on the thirteenth."

"You shouldn't have done that, Hester," said Debby. "If you didn't know, you shouldn't have answered it."

"I suppose I shouldn't have done so," said Hester. "I did not intend to do so, Aunt Debby. I did not know then that we were to write on our paper whether we had given or received help. I really did it thoughtlessly."

"A girl fifteen years old has a right to think," responded Debby Alden, grimly. "Thinking about what you do is part of your business." That was all the encouragement she received from Debby Alden.

Miss Watson continued her story. When she said that Hester had refused to turn tale-bearer, Debby's face lighted up. The words gave her a sense of relief. She turned to Hester. "I'm glad you wrote what was true across your paper. It would have been wrong to do anything else, and I'm glad you didn't tell on that other person. I don't like the idea of your being disobedient, but you shouldn't have told. I don't know whether any one had a right to ask that of you. Come, get your wraps, Hester, and we'll go home."

At this, Mr. Sanderson walked through the room. He recognized Miss Alden as Debby's legal protector, for the story of the child's adoption was widely known.

"I trust, Miss Alden, that you have heard the truth about Miss Hester's disobedience and dishonesty."

Debby Alden arose, and with the native dignity and self-possession which were always with her, replied: "I've been told that you couldn't compel her to turn talebearer. I'm glad of it. There's nothing that is dishonest in keeping such matters to yourself. Come, Hester. Bid Miss Watson good evening."

She left the room, followed by Hester's three girl friends. Jane discussed the matter freely; Orpha listened in her own heavy, dull way, while Mary Bowerman walked along on the other edge of the group and had nothing at all to say.

"I'm afraid mother will not like my staying so long," said Jane, "but she will not care when I tell her the reason. I had no intention of leaving that room until I saw what was going to be done with you."

"I was getting afraid when Professor said I should stay there until I told. It would have been dreadful to stay there alone all night."

"But you wouldn't be alone," said Jane. "Do you think that I would go home and leave you there? Well, hardly. I was doing some thinking, Hester, while you and Mr. Sanderson were talking. I had my plans well made."

"What would you have done, Jane?" She slipped one arm through Jane's; the other was already clinging tight about her Aunt Debby.

"I thought that Miss Watson would not go home and leave you alone, but if she

did, I meant to stay. I meant to have
Mary leave word at home to send us something to eat. We wouldn't have had such
a dreadful night, Hester. We could have
had our lunch and read the library books,
and then — well, the benches would not
have been the softest cots in the world.
But," with a smile, "I suppose when one is
tired, one doesn't think much of the bed."

"I think it would be dreadful to stay
there all night," began Hester. She now
feared the thought of it more than she had
feared the possibility.

"But you wouldn't have told, even if you
were afraid?" asked Jane.

"Never. I'll never tell. If Professor Sanderson would have kept me there for a
week I would not have told."

"Why?" asked Orpha. She raised her
dull, expressionless eyes to Hester. It was
impossible for Orpha to grasp that subtle
difference between action actuated by a
high sense of honor and that which was not.

"Because," replied Jane, quickly. "Isn't that an excellent reason, Orpha? She wouldn't because she wouldn't." Jane had long since learned how worse than wasted were those explanations which were given to Orpha.

"I suppose Professor Sanderson will not go from his way to be good to me, after what has happened," said Hester. A pained expression came to her eyes for an instant. She was an affectionate girl, to whom the love and kindness of those with whom she lived and those with whom she worked at school were necessary for her happiness. During these last two months she had seen enough of Professor Sanderson to realize that she could never again be in his good books. The thought hurt her. But, determined not to show how much the experience she had gone through had affected her, she said with assumed carelessness: "But, Miss Watson will be there. So long as we have her, we can go along without Professor

Sanderson's good-will. But, nevertheless, I'm glad that I do not recite to him."

"It will blow over in a day or so. You will forget it, and so will he. Don't you think so, Miss Debby?" asked Jane.

"I don't know. I hope so," she replied.

"I'm sure it will not," said Hester. "I remember just ordinary occurrences longer than that; I know I shall never forget this."

"You think so now." Jane smiled blandly. She had found the touchstone of happiness. She always managed to turn the darkest cloud about until she caught a glimpse of its silver lining.

"I see plainly how the matter will end. That other party to the transaction will hear of what took place this evening, and then she'll walk up like a lady and plead guilty. Don't you think so, Mary?" She turned to Mary, who was lagging along on the outer edge of the line, several steps behind the others.

"How do I know? I haven't listened to a word you were saying."

"Well, that is flattering. All my flow of eloquence wasted!" She looked back over her shoulder as she continued: "Why don't you come and walk with us? There's plenty of room on these wide pavements, and we're not apt to meet any one this time in the evening." Then, as Mary did not respond to her invitation, she continued: "What's the trouble? You've been glum for the last hour. I haven't heard you say a word since we left school."

"There wouldn't have been much chance, if I'd wanted to."

"I'll keep quiet. Speak up. I promise I will not say another word unless you ask me." There was always good-humor in Jane's voice and manner. In all the school-girl spats, she met the most ill-natured remarks with apparent good-nature. Now she but smiled again, as Mary retorted: "Don't try it. You'd go into convulsions if you couldn't do all the talking."

Hester alone understood the reason for

Mary's lack of interest in the conversation. She was disappointed in her friend. She knew that Mary was sharp in her way of speaking, but she had always believed her upright and honorable. But the occurrences of the day had proved that she was neither. She meant to tell Mary plainly what she thought of such conduct, but she could not do so in the presence of others. She decided to wait and create an opportunity of seeing her alone on the morrow.

One by one the girls left Debby and Hester, and the last of their walk was alone. Debby did not again bring up the subject of the trouble in school. She was vexed with Hester that the girl had taken help from any one; on the other hand, she was pleased that no denial had been made of this, and that Hester had taken such a stand with regard to giving information. So the matter was equalized. The supper had been almost spoiled from waiting so long, yet both were so hungry that they could

have relished less palatable fare. During
the meal Debby kept up the conversation,
for the reaction had begun with Hester, and
she was nervous and depressed.

Debby would not allow her to talk of
school, and kept the conversation to the
trifling matters of the house and some new
shirt-waists which they were making. She
was not a little curious about the girl who
had been party to giving help in class, yet
she would not ask Hester to tell her.

"It's no use of my knowing," she repeated to herself. "No good will come of
it. I might tell before I was aware of
what I was saying. Then, too, I'd dislike
a girl who wouldn't be honest. I'd dislike
her doubly because it was my Hester who
was harmed by her not telling. I suppose
it isn't right to feel so, but it's natural."

She hurried with the supper work, Hester
drying the dishes, while her aunt washed
them. When the work was finished, Hester
took out her books, but Debby stopped her.

"We're not going to study one speck
this night," she said decidedly. "I'll work
a spell at those waists, and you can read.
We'll not stay up. We're both tuckered
out, and I mean that we shall be in bed
early."

Hester was pleased with this arrange-
ment. She was tired. She took up a book,
but could not fix her mind upon it. In
spite of her efforts, her thoughts went back
to the events of the afternoon. Before a
half-hour had passed, she laid aside her book
and suggested that they go to bed.

She thought to meet Mary Bowerman
on the way to school the next morning,
but that young lady had been wise and had
been gone from home some time when Hester passed the Bowermans'. When Hester
entered the class room, Mary was in her
seat, studying so diligently that she neither
spoke nor raised her head as Hester passed
her. At noon she was the first to leave
and the last to enter for the afternoon

session. She seemed as anxious to avoid
being alone with Hester as the latter was to
meet her.

During the middle of the afternoon
session Mary walked into the cloak-room.
As quickly as she could be excused, Hester
was with her. Mary turned quickly when
she heard the door close. Recognizing Hester, she was about to leave the room, but
Hester detained her. "Wait one moment,
Mary. I must speak to you."

"I haven't time. I'll see you after
school. I must get out my geometry."
She spoke with careless indifference, which,
however, did not deceive her companion
into believing that she was wholly uncon-
cerned. She again moved toward the door,
but Hester was before her. Standing with
her back against the door, she looked squarely
at Mary.

"I wish to know why you didn't write
on your examination paper that you, too,
had received help."

Mary tilted back her head. "It seems to me that that is my business, Hester Alden."

"It is partly my business. You heard what took place last evening. Why didn't you tell then?"

"What is it to you? You were not punished on my account. You —"

"You heard what Professor Sanderson said to me. He would have punished me severely if Miss Watson had not come to my help."

"But not on my account. He did that because you were so obstinate. If you had told him when he asked you at first, the matter would have ended there."

"Did you wish me to tell? If you were so indifferent to consequences, why did you not tell him that you were the other party?"

"You seemed to have some particular reason for keeping it a secret. My telling would not have helped matters for you. Professor Sanderson was punishing you for

your obstinacy. Don't put the blame of
it on me."

Hester stood and looked at Mary. She
could not understand such a nature. She
had played with Mary Bowerman since the
primary days, and thought that she knew
her so well.

"Did you wish me to tell?" she asked
again.

"I have nothing to say about what you
do. Suit yourself. I suppose, though,
you'll do the heroic part and have Miss
Watson fuss over you. She's treated you
to-day as though you were too precious for
everyday use, and should be kept under a
glass case. Tell? Why, you wouldn't tell
if I'd get down on my knees and beg you
to. You enjoy playing the heroic too well.
No," with a disdainful toss of her head as
though by that motion she cast the matter
from her, "I have nothing to say about
what you'll do."

"I have something to say about what

you'll do, Mary Bowerman." Hester spoke decidedly. "If you have one spark of honor, one little mite of self-respect left, you'll go to Professor Sanderson this very day and tell him that I wrote out the imperative mode for you."

"See me do it. Get away from that door, Hester Alden, and let me go back to the room. I haven't glanced at my geometry yet."

"I'll not get away from the door until I'm through talking, and I'm not through yet, Mary Bowerman. I'll not be through until I tell you what I think of you."

Mary gave a disdainful toss of her head and twisted her mouth into an expression of weariness. She leaned against the wall as she said, indifferently: "Well, proceed. When words fail you, consult the dictionary in the next room. But remember, Hester, what Miss Warner has taught you in composition. When in doubt, cut out adjectives."

Her tones and expression were galling. Hester's eyes flashed. She began to speak quickly, hurriedly, and in anger. "I think you are mean and dishonorable. You've cheated and lied about it, and you've treated me disagreeably, and insulted me because I would not betray you. You are the most deceitful person I know. I'll never call you friend again. I'll never speak to you as long as I live." She caught herself quickly, for Aunt Debby's training asserted itself. "Yes, I'll speak to you. I didn't mean that I never would. But it will be weeks and weeks before I do. I mean every word I said about despising you."

"Who cares if you speak or not? You have such a temper and flare up so, that it's hardly safe to be where you are. As to speaking to me, you should be glad and thankful if I or any other nice girl notice you. You're nothing but a tramp baby."

Hester's eyes opened wide. This was

new to her. "What do you mean? Tell me how you dare say such a thing, Mary Bowerman."

"I dare say it, because it's true. Your mother was tramping through the country when she was killed. If Miss Debby Alden hadn't taken pity on you, you'd have been sent to the county home."

There was a ring of conviction in this speech that impressed Hester. She gazed at Mary with a shocked, startled look. She had neither voice nor words to reply to this. Mary saw the effect of her words, and took advantage of it.

"You don't intend to notice me. You have no idea how funny that sounds. Why, the only reason that I and the other girls ever had anything at all to do with you is that we pitied you. But now we'll cut you. Remember, Hester Alden, you need never expect to go with me and my friends."

Hester had unconsciously moved away from the door. Mary, seeing her opportunity, hurried from the room. As she left, she looked back over her shoulder and laughed tauntingly.

Left alone, Hester stood leaning against the wall. She was dazed. She could not return to the schoolroom. She wished to think about what Mary had said, yet she could not think, for everything was mixed up in her brain, and the room moved uncertain before her.

CHAPTER VII

HESTER ALDEN was absent from the geometry class, which recited to Mr. Wilbur. This teacher was new to the ways of high school. He inquired for Miss Alden, and no one volunteering information, the subject was dismissed. The freshmen Latin followed the geometry. Miss Watson, who had taken charge of that department, was alert. She at once missed Miss Alden, but asked no information in general concerning her. On the contrary, she turned to Jane with the question, "Miss Orr, where is Miss Alden?"

"She went into the cloak-room before geometry class. She had not returned when the class came over."

That was all for that time. Miss Watson gave them work to keep them employed. Then, unobserved, she went into the cloak-room. Hester stood just as Mary had left her almost an hour before. Her head was against the wall, while her hand clasped the coat rack for support.

"What is the trouble? Are you ill, Hester?"

She raised her head and looked at Miss Watson.

"I don't know," she said wearily. "I think I must be."

"Go to the teachers' room and lie down. When you feel better, you may go home. I'll explain to the other teachers." She was alarmed by the pallor of Hester's face and the peculiarly dazed expression of her eyes.

The girl made an attempt to obey, but the room moved about her. She threw out her arms to steady herself. Miss Watson came to her assistance. Throwing her arms about her, Hester leaned her head against her and sobbed aloud. Miss Watson let her have her cry out, and then said: "Something from the ordinary has happened, Hester. Can you tell me what it is?"

"No, Miss Watson. I've heard something that troubled me. It made me ill."

Perhaps Miss Watson had a suspicion what that something was. She knew Hester's story. She had spent her life with young girls, and read them better than they suspected.

"I should not allow myself to be troubled by what I heard. There are many things repeated that are not worth a thought. Don't allow yourself to be disturbed by such matters. You must bear in mind that much of what one hears is not the truth. Perhaps what has disturbed you may not have a grain of truth in it."

Hester raised her head. "Perhaps it hasn't, but it sounded like the truth. She surely would not have dared to say such things if they were not true."

Miss Watson had no idea to whom she referred. "Some people dare do anything," she said. "I must return to my class. Remain in the teachers' room until you feel better." With this advice she was gone. Hester went into the teachers' room, but could not lie down. She stood by the window, her head pressed against the cool pane. She went over all that Mary had said, and she brought to mind all the little incidents and suggestions that had been given her concerning her mother's death.

Aunt Debby had told her very little. She knew that her mother had been killed at the crossing, and that she was buried at Fairview. Aunt Debby had taken her to see the grave. The granite slab had upon it only the date of her mother's death. There was neither date of birth nor name.

"It must be true," she said. "Aunt Debby didn't know her age and name. No one knew. Aunt Debby just took me in." Then a new thought came to her in connection with Debby Alden. Like a flash

there spread out before the girl's eyes the
long stretch of sixteen years of kindness
and care that this woman had given her.
It helped her to bear the loss of name and
mother. "Wasn't that noble of Aunt
Debby?" she said to herself, while her
heart gave a leap of joy, "and I hadn't one
little bit of claim upon her."

As she looked at the subject with this
new knowledge before her, she felt that
Mary Bowerman had told the truth. She
really belonged to no one, and the name
Alden in which she had taken so much
pride was not her own. She was naturally
of a happy disposition. She could not be
depressed long. Her youth and vitality
asserted itself, and before the time for the
closing of the day's session had come, she
was outwardly herself again.

Entering the schoolroom, she put her
books in order, and then spoke to Jane,
asking her to wait to walk home with her.
She felt as though she could not treat Mary

courteously if they were together, and she did not wish to be alone.

Jane lingered in the cloak-room. Mary was deliberate about arranging her books, so that the greater number of pupils had gone before she was ready. Hester hurried after Jane. "I'm ready now, Jane. Come on."

"Let us wait for Mary. She'll be here in a minute. She and Orpha will come together." Then Hester replied, as she observed the surprised look, "Mary and I had a little spat to-day. I do not wish to walk home with her until, — well, until I feel differently toward her."

"Oh, very well." Jane turned and came with her. She asked no questions about the cause of the difficulty. A proper regard for other persons' affairs had been bred in her. If Hester saw fit to tell her about the trouble with Mary, well and good, but if she did not, Jane had no thought of asking impertinent questions.

The two walked home together, talking
freely of every subject of common interest
except the difficulty with Mary Bowerman.

Hester had part of her walk alone, as
Jane lived just at the edge of town. Aunt
Debby was standing at the gate waiting
for her. Hester saw her at a distance and
waved. Debby Alden returned the salute
with interest. As Hester came closer, she
saw the woman in a new light. Debby
Alden had improved since the day she
had had her heart-to-heart talk with Miss
Richards fully ten years before. Her life
had grown fuller and broader, and every
expression of her face, every movement,
gave testimony to it.

Her hair was drawn softly from her forehead. The stern expression of her eyes
had given place to a tender one. Her soft
white waist was dainty and becoming.
She had lost nothing of her strength and
individuality, but to them she had added a
gentle sweetness and consideration.

"I was tempted to wait and walk home with you," she said, as Hester came near. "I have been in town the greater part of the day. Mrs. Orr and I went shopping this morning, and we had our club meeting this afternoon."

"Did you have a good time?" asked Hester, entering the gate. Her voice had a new touch to it which did not escape Debby Alden. She turned and looked keenly at Hester, but there was nothing in the girl's expression to cause alarm. Thus reassured, she replied to Hester's question, "Yes, I did have a good time. Perhaps it was because I enjoyed the work. You know I was to read a paper on myths and folk-lore. I read it to you several weeks ago. The ladies declared it was fine, and wondered how I found time to devote so much time to research." She laughed, and Hester joined her.

"Did you tell them, Aunt Debby, that it had taken you ten years to write that paper?"

"No, I did not, Hester. I'm afraid they would have doubted it if I had."

"Yet it is true."

"Yes, but I'm afraid they would not have understood. It has been just ten years; for you were five when Miss Richards gave me the book to find stories for you. That was the first, and we've not neglected it since."

"But they've grown harder, Aunt Debby. You have no idea what a help in the classics my knowing them has been. I never need look up the allusions. Miss Leonard complimented me upon knowing them, and Miss Watson says that knowing the Greek and Latin myths will be a great help when we begin to read Virgil."

They were walking toward the house. Hester had her arm about Debby Alden's waist. The girl felt that she must show her affection and gratitude in some way. Had she had her way, she would have expressed her love in no weak words, and would have told Debby Alden how she appreciated the care and self-sacrifice that she had given her. But to have said a word on the subject would disclose the fact that Hester knew what Aunt Debby wished kept from her.

"If Aunt Debby wished me to know," reasoned Hester, "she would have told me. I shall never let her know what Mary has told me."

"Virgil," repeated Debby. "The word sounds difficult. I'm afraid that I shall never be able to read it. Perhaps you can manage that alone, Hester."

"Oh, Aunt Debby, don't give it up. Miss Watson says that we're just now in the drudgery of Latin, and that the pleasure will come when we begin reading the stories. You will not give it up, Aunt Debby?"

"We'll not decide until next fall, Hester. That will be time enough." The beginner's work in Latin had been difficult for her.

Hester did not realize how hard the woman studied to keep up with her. However, one strong point was in her favor; while the lessons were difficult to acquire, she was able to retain them.

"Supper is not ready," said Debby, as they entered the kitchen. "But we'll take our time. There is no need to hurry, since to-day's Friday and there'll be no lessons this evening."

"I'll arrange the table," said Hester. Without waiting, she began to assist her Aunt Debby. She had it in mind to be a help and a comfort to the one who had befriended her. She watched herself closely and did all things as Debby Alden wished them done. When supper was finished, she helped with the dishes, and never before had the china such a polishing as it had this particular evening. Suddenly she paused, with a plate in one hand and the drying towel in the other. "I've just begun to realize how much you've done for me, Aunt Debby. I suppose I'll never be able to repay you."

"Who has ever said anything about being paid? It wasn't for that I brought you up." She spoke sharply.

"I know that, yet I'd be ungrateful if I didn't realize what you've done for me and what sacrifices you've made. I was thinking about it to-day while I was in school, and I made up my mind then that the best I could do would never make matters quite even between us. I want to be a great help and comfort to you, Aunt Debby."

"The greatest comfort you can be to me now is to get your lessons well in school, and be honest and truthful. I hate a sneak and a liar. I never could understand why the Lord let them cumber the earth." She spoke sternly. Hester did not remember the time when she had heard her aunt speak in just that way. There was a touch of fierceness in her voice that awed the girl. But she said simply: "I'll try, then, to be a comfort to you, Aunt Debby. I'll get the best reports I can. As to ever being a sneak or a liar, I do not believe I could be either, Aunt Debby, if I tried."

She put the plates in the corner of the cupboard, rinsed out the drying towel, and sat down near her aunt. The kitchen clock striking the hour aroused her to her surroundings. "Half-past eight. We surely are late. I think, Aunt Debby, I will go to bed if you do not need me, and do not mind sitting alone."

"Are you sick, Hester?"

"No; I'm not just sick, but I do not feel like myself. I did not feel well in school. I stayed in the teachers' room and missed two classes."

"You'd better go to bed, then. I'll be up in a few minutes. You must keep warm. You'd better put blankets on your bed. Get those gray ones from the chest."

When Hester had gone from the kitchen,

Debby Alden went out to the wash-house in search of her unfailing remedy, a fire-brick, which she put on top of the kitchen stove to heat. When it was hot, she wrapped it up in newspapers, and carried it upstairs to Hester's room.

Pulling up the covers from the foot of the bed, she placed the hot brick at Hester's feet.

"If you've taken cold, that will keep you from being chilled. Keeping warm, or having a good sweat, is the best thing for either a cold or a fever." She tucked down the bedclothes, and then turned her attention to the girl's head.

"You haven't a speck of fever," she said, laying her hand on Hester's head. "I suppose it's just a 'brashy' spell. We must watch our eating to-morrow. That's what has caused the trouble."

"Are you coming to bed now, Aunt Debby?"

"Not for a spell yet. I'm going downstairs again." She went back to the kitchen, and, making herself comfortable in the great wooden rocker, with her feet upon the hearth of the stove, she began to piece together the incidents of the day to see what she could make of them as a whole. She knew it was not natural for a girl Hester's age to speak about repaying her. Some one had set the child thinking along a new line, and Debby Alden made up her mind there and then that she would find out who that was and put a stop to it.

It was a common saying throughout the locality that Debby Alden was no one's fool. Her keenness of intuition, and the logic that showed in her reasoning, now proved that her reputation was well-founded. She thought of the trouble of the day before. She knew Hester well enough to know that she would speak sharply and frankly to the girl whom she had helped in the examination, and who was not honest enough to confess it. It would

be natural for the girl to answer back. No
doubt, a war of words followed. Hester
had felt sick afterward, and then this great
desire to be a comfort and help to Aunt
Debby who had done so much for her.
To Debby Alden the whole matter was as
clear as an open book. She meant to find
out who that girl was, and see to it that she
would not again hector Hester with her
suggestions and hints. She must be one
who knew Hester well, or they would not
have helped each other. She brought to
mind each of the girls with whom Hester
was friendly. Jane Orr was not to be
thought of. Debby remembered with pleasure the speech that Jane had made the
evening before. As she thought of that
walk home, she was suddenly enlightened as
to the guilty party. She remembered how
Mary had kept on the outer edge of the
group, how sullen and silent she had been,
without a civil word for any one.

"And it isn't generally Mary Bower-

man's way not to talk. She's generally
ready with a word on her tongue. Kate
was always the most ambitious, envious
person hereabouts. 'Mother and daughter
alike,' is an old saying. I've noticed that
before in Kate and Mary. I'm thinking
that I've found the right person now, and
I'll see to it that she doesn't nag Hester. I
will not have it."

She did not for an instant suspect that
Mary Bowerman had told Hester the truth.
She did not know that Mary herself knew
it. She took it for granted that Mary had
gone no further in her annoyance than
merely hinting. Debby did not decide just
what course she would pursue in the matter,
but she experienced a feeling of relief in
knowing that she had found the culprit.
She was quite ready to sleep now. She
slipped into Hester's room and found her
sleeping. She did considerable thinking and
planning the following morning, as she prepared breakfast. Before the morning's

work was well under way, she had reached a decision.

"Mrs. Bowerman is going into town this morning, Hester," she said. "I wish you would go with her and ask Miss Richards for the book she promised me. It's about taking charge of club meetings. You had better go now, for Mrs. Bowerman is never slack about starting when she means to go."

She noticed Hester's face flush and the hesitancy in her manner as she answered: "Yes, Aunt Debby. But I do not mind the walk alone. I rather enjoy being by myself sometimes."

"But I don't wish you to. There's always strangers coming and going, and no one knows who they are. I'd feel safer if you have company, and Kate is going. She told me so."

There was nothing to do but obey. Hester put on her wraps and started forth, not at all pleased with the prospect of meeting Mary Bowerman in her own home.

Debby Alden finished the morning's work, and then started for the Bowerman home. She knew that Kate and Hester had long since left the house. Going around to the back door, which was a custom of the neighborhood, she entered the kitchen, which Mary had just put in order.

"No, I shall not sit down," she said grimly, in reply to Mary's invitation.

"Mother has gone to town, Miss Debby. She'll be back in the course of a half-hour. You'd better sit down while you are waiting."

"I'll not wait to see your mother. I didn't come to see her. It is you I wish to see."

"Me?" said Mary, indifferent alike to grammar and Miss Debby's purpose in coming.

"Yes, you. I came to tell you that you are not to hector Hester with your taunts and insinuations."

"Did Hester run to you and tell? I do declare that I'm surprised after the hero she tried to make of herself before Mr. Sanderson."

"No; Hester did not tell. She was never a girl to carry tales about, and she hasn't begun it now. Hester doesn't know that I know about what happened yesterday, or about you getting help in your examinations. It doesn't matter how I know, but it does matter that you are to keep a civil tongue in your head with Hester. You may have all the schoolgirl squabbles you wish. Hester can take care of herself; but you're not to tell her about her mother's death or her people."

As she spoke, Mary's mind went over the events of the previous day. Who could have told Miss Debby? The only person who could possibly know of the talk between herself and Hester was Miss Watson. She hastily concluded that it was Miss Watson, and Mary feared her and knew that such conduct, if it were known, would meet with punishment.

"Do you understand?" Debby Alden again asked.

"Yes; I understand. I'm sure that I'll not bother my head at all about Hester, Miss Debby. You do not need to be at all concerned."

"Well, see that you keep to that," were Debby's parting words. There were few whom she could not inspire with awe when in this mood. She left the Bowerman home with the feeling that she had settled the matter for a time, yet she knew that the story was too well-known and too interesting to be forgotten. She realized, also, that Hester might always be exposed to experiences similar to that of the previous day. Debby Alden could not bear the thought that Hester would suffer from such remarks. She knew that the child's sensitive nature would make her peculiarly susceptible to suffering.

CHAPTER VIII

DURING the first week of December the weather grew intensely cold. There had been no wind such as usually marked the winter months in the valley. There had been a full September flood in the river and plenty of rain during that month and October; so when the cold weather set in, the river was not low. The rocks in the river-bed near the end of the town were covered by a foot of water — just enough to prevent the 'riffles.'

The difference of six inches, more or less, was an important matter to the young and active element of the town. They read the signs well, and watched the indications for high or low water and no wind, with intense interest. The skating depended entirely upon such conditions. If the ice was formed while a stiff breeze swept the surface of the river, or when the water was so low that it made little rippling circles as it passed over the rocks, the skating was ruined for that season. But now, after several days and nights of still, bitter weather, the matter was settled for months. For miles the main portion of the stream was one unbroken sheet of ice, as clear and smooth as glass, and thick enough so that the skaters took no risks.

Friday morning Jane Orr came into the cloak-room where a half-dozen of her friends were leisurely removing their wraps. It was generally understood that the pupils should not congregate here, but as communication was forbidden within the school-room proper, the girls were most deliberate about removing and arranging their wraps, especially on those mornings when some one of the number had a long story to tell.

Jane's face was wreathed with smiles as she joined the girls. She began talking as she removed her tam-o'-shanter in order that none of the precious minutes might be lost. Although she talked rapidly, her voice never lost its low, deliberate tones. "Oh, girls! I have the best news! I could scarcely wait until I reached here to tell you. I'm all out of breath. You'll be as glad to hear it as I was." Here she jammed her hat pins through the crown of the tam, and, with it in her hand, turned about and faced her half-dozen listeners.

"Ralphie and some of his young men friends skated to Hyner last evening. It was moonlight, you know. Ralphie said that the ice was fine — simply fine! That for the entire six miles there wasn't a break."

A sigh of satisfaction came from her listeners. They had been disappointed the year before, and for weeks they had hoped for and counted much upon good ice for skating.

"We can't go to-night after school," said one of the group. "No one has brought skates. By the time we go home for them, it will be too late. Mine must be sharpened before I use them. They're saw-toothed on the edge."

"I wasn't through with what I was going to say," cried Jane. "Ralphie said that we must not on any account miss the skate. So he suggested getting up a crowd of girls for to-morrow afternoon, to start immediately after dinner."

"It will be so cold," said Orpha.

"Of course it will," said Edith, "but is a little cold going to hurt us?"

"You will not wait until I finish," said Jane. She had taken off her coat by this time, and had seated herself on the extreme edge of a small bench. "We can get a warm supper at Hyner before we start to skate back. That will keep us from getting cold while we rest."

"If it's hard skating against the wind, we can come back on the evening train," said Janet, who was always practical. "I

wouldn't mind going down, but the skate
back with the wind against one is too hard."

"Ralphie will go along so that nothing
can happen. If one of us should fall, he's
big and strong enough to take care of us."
Here Jane's bland smile fairly outdid itself,
for, in her mind, if there were one person
in the world who was absolutely faultless,
that person was her elder brother Ralph.

"Who'll go?" asked Janet. "And
where'll we meet, and at what time?"

The seven girls who were present all
declared themselves willing and ready, de-
barring a little sharpening of skates, which
could be attended to the following morning.

"A dozen is just a nice party," said Janet.

"Della will go, I'm sure, and Julia. I'll
ask them this morning."

"And Hester," said Jane. "She'll go, of
course. I'll speak to her while we're going
into algebra. She's always just ahead of
me in the line."

"Oh!" said Mary Bowerman, and then

waited without further word. Her tone was so expressive of dissatisfaction at Jane's suggestion, that the other six girls looked up at her in surprise, and then waited for her to speak. Seeing what was expected of her, she continued: "Must we ask her? I'd so much rather that she wouldn't be one of the crowd."

"Why?" asked Janet, who never took such subtle suggestions, but demanded point-blank statements.

"I do not know that it is necessary for me to give my reasons," Mary replied. "I know that I don't wish to have her."

"I do," said Jane, sweetly but firmly. "And I see no reason why she should not be invited. I'm sure she is always agreeable, and she never keeps one waiting, and she will not hang back and say that she's tired and wants to rest. You know that she will not complain and grumble, whatever happens."

"Well, if Hester Alden is one of the

party, I will not be," said Mary, decidedly. She had intended keeping the promise which she made to Miss Alden some weeks before. She tried to reconcile her conscience by telling herself that this was not hectoring Hester; that she was saying no word to her. Yet she knew what it was Miss Alden meant, and that so far she had fulfilled the letter and not the spirit of the promise. After this declaration about not going, she waited a moment to see what effect her words would have on the girls. If she expected protestations and beseechings on their part, she was disappointed. Her declaration was followed by silence. She repeated her words, making them as emphatic as possible.

"Well, I'll tell you this. If Hester Alden goes, I will not."

"You must suit yourself about that," Jane replied. "I intend to ask Hester."

She had unconsciously moved closer to the edge of the seat as she talked. A footstep was heard in the hall. With the thought that a teacher was coming to take them to task for their loitering, the two girls, who had been occupying the greater portion of the bench, sprang to their feet. With Jane, plump and round as a partridge, on the unsupported end of the bench, a state of equilibrium could not be maintained. The bench tilted, and Jane sat unexpectedly upon the floor.

She made no effort to rise, but remained there laughing heartily at her plight. The door opened and Hester came in.

"The halls were so quiet that I was afraid I was late," she said. Then, seeing Jane sitting upon the floor, she exclaimed: "For all the world, Jane Orr! Why are you sitting there?"

"I've been issuing invitations to a skating party, and this is the way it affected me. You're invited, Hester. When I get the dust from my dress, I'll tell you all about it." She was on her feet by this time, brushing vigorously at the coat of tan, which showed against the dark blue skirt.

The others of the party turned to leave the cloak-room, when Jane called after them: "Meet at our house at one-thirty. Don't forget to bring money along to pay for your supper. It's to be a Dutch treat."

Then she turned to Hester and told her of the arrangements for the following afternoon.

"I'll go if I can," Hester replied, "but I'm not sure about my skates. They were too small for me two years ago, and I wear shoes two sizes larger than I did then. But if I can possibly use them, I'll be there."

The following morning after breakfast she went to the attic to look for her skates. She did not doubt that her Aunt Debby would gladly buy her a larger pair if she knew that the old ones were too small. But since Mary Bowerman had told her the facts of Debby Alden's giving her a home, Hester could not ask for luxuries.

It was quite enough to be clothed and fed.

The skates were packed in one of the great boxes in which the attic was rich. Hester looked through several. One of these contained each article of clothing which her mother had worn when she was killed. Debby Alden had put them in order and packed them away. She understood now why her aunt had been careful to save the most insignificant of these.

"Poor Aunt Debby," said Hester to herself, "I suppose she thought that some one might come to claim me, and she wanted to identify my mother and me. That is why she keeps that little old dress of mine."

She examined the waist and skirt critically, yet without any sign of emotion.

"My mother could not have been a tramp. These clothes are fine — nicer than Debby's best dress, and they are the kind that a lady would wear."

She replaced each article as she had found it. She was displeased with herself that she had not felt sad and cried. But she had not. If the stories she had read could be relied upon, her indifferent feeling was quite unnatural. The feeling of tenderness was all for Aunt Debby, and not for this strange unknown woman which Mary Bowerman had declared was her mother.

"Maybe I haven't any heart," she said. "If I had, I suppose I'd cry and be sad, but I do not feel at all like it. Where are those skates?" She began searching through the fourth box. Before she was aware of what she was doing, she was singing a cheerful song.

Debby Alden had come upstairs, and, hearing Hester fussing about, came to the foot of the attic stairs and called up: "Hester, what are you doing up there? Now don't get those boxes in disorder."

"I'm not, auntie. I'm putting everything back. I was looking for my skates, but I've found them now."

She came down the dark, narrow stairway, the skates clinking in her hand. Sitting down on the lower step, she raised her foot and put the skate on it. It was fully two inches shorter than the shoe.

"Too short," said Debby Alden, laconically. "Yes, I thought they'd be. When did you mean to use them?"

"This afternoon, if they were all right. But I hardly expected that they would be. I've grown so since these were new."

"Do the girls intend to go?"

"Yes." Then before Hester realized what she was doing, she told her aunt, just as Debby Alden wished her to do.

"You had better go to Ab Stout's right off and get a pair. You should get a fairly good pair for two dollars."

"I can do without them, Aunt Debby. We'd better not spend the money. You said just the other day that you'd have to save a little."

"I can spend two dollars. I never let myself get as close as that. That was never the Alden way. We always keep a little saved back. Besides, I meant right along to get you skates for Christmas."

That settled the matter. Hester lost no time in getting into her wraps and setting out for Stout's department store.

It was a busy time in all departments, for Saturday morning was a general shopping day. Farmers' wives, who had come to town on the market wagons, were laying in a week's supply of groceries; miners' wives from Bitumen were there in groups of six and eight, and the keen Joel Stout, the junior member of the firm, was beguiling them to part with their money for light, shoddy wraps, and head-gear conspicuous for its long, light plumes and quantities of flowers.

Hester made her way through the

crowd to the household department, where skates held their place with pots, pans, and waffle-irons. This department was not so crowded, yet she was compelled to wait some time before she could have the services of a clerk.

Abner Stout himself had charge of this department. Esther and Mary, two of his younger children, assisted him. Business had prospered with the man. He could boast no nationality or trade. He was a hybrid, sprung from the sharpest, keenest, and most unprincipled types of several nationalities. In his early days he had been a junk and rag dealer. He had failed as often as the law permitted, and each failure added to the money he had hoarded away, so that he was at last enabled to start in business on his present substantial scale. He had cut communications with all his old friends, for he knew of nothing to be gained by a further acquaintance with them. He had passed the place where they could be used by him as stepping-stones, and he had no wish to serve the purpose of a stepping-stone to them. His trade had grown so large that every member of the family was kept busy handling it. His daughters had no time to give to domestic matters, and for weeks housekeeping and cooking had gone by the board. The family had eaten at odd minutes, helping themselves to cheese and crackers or a dried herring as they passed from one department to another.

This way of living was not pleasing to the elder man. He liked a well-laid table with plenty of good, strong fare, but business was business, and his daughters were needed as clerks. He might have employed one of the townspeople as clerk, but his economical soul revolted at the thought. It was not so much the salary that constrained him from employing such a one, but Joel and he had little ways of their own in weighing and measuring, and marking up and down, a system that was hard for the mind of some to grasp.

In the midst of his difficulties an excellent plan presented itself to his mind for consideration. There was living in New York one Jane Farwell, an elder sister of his deceased wife. Jane was making her home with her brother Reuben, a dealer in junk and rags to whom she had been a great help, for she was quick to sort. But she was not content, as the work was tedious and the stooping stiffened her back, and, besides, Reuben grew angry if she so much as mentioned wages and declared that she was a burden upon him.

This Jane Farwell had been an excellent housekeeper in her younger day, being trained after the fashion of the thrifty housewife, and she knew much about the cooking of food along economical lines.

He decided to send for Jane. She could keep the house in order and make ready the meals, and she would be glad to come for little or nothing. He wrote to her. His heart grew glad when she sent word that she would come. This had occurred three weeks before, and for almost that length of time Jane had been in his kitchen preparing the savory messes whose strong, fragrant odor filled the shop and lingered for days. It was little wonder, then, that he was in the best of humor and laughed and joked with his customers. His little sharp gray eyes glistened like polished beads, his sharp thin nose was elevated beyond its usual angle, and his hands with their long talons and sharp-pointed nails rubbed together, expressive of his greatest satisfaction; for the presence of his sister-in-law, Jane, in the kitchen, preparing savory dishes and without a word as to wages, was as oil and myrrh to his covetous soul.

Kate Bowerman and Mrs. Mullin had come shopping together. They were both keen at a bargain, and enjoyed being to-

gether when buying was on hand. Mary
Stout was waiting upon them. They had
made their selections and were waiting
while she put together their purchases and
made the change. Abner stood at a distance, with eye and ear seizing upon all
that took place in his store.

At this instant Hester entered, and, passing the women, went on to the counter
where skates were laid out. Her long coat
of dark blue was brightened by a crimson
tam-o'-shanter and the crimson bow at
the end of her long, dark braid.

Mrs. Mullin nudged her companion. "A
fine-looking girl," she said in stage whispers.

"Think so?" said Kate Bowerman. She
gave forth a mirthless cackle. "I suppose she's good-looking to them who like
that style. I don't and never did. A
woman or girl to be good-looking should be
fair."

"I don't agree with you, Kate. I'm
all for dark eyes and dark hair." She

turned and looked at the girlish figure bending over the counter on which lay the skates.

"It must cost Debby Alden a pretty penny to dress her. I see her go by the house on her way to school, and she's as well dressed as any girl in town. Better than Debby Alden ever dressed. I wonder that Debby does it, for you know yourself that the Aldens were always counted close. I wouldn't have believed it if any one would have told me! Debby Alden spending her folks' money on a strange child."

Abner Stout drew nearer. To all outward appearances, his attention was wrapped up in the sale of a butcher knife, over the price of which an old German woman was haggling. He believed in learning all he could of other people's business, so he drew closer to the two women.

Kate gave a malicious laugh, and for an instant the point of her tongue showed between her lips.

"Debby Alden's no one's fool, Hattie Mullin. You've heard that time and time again, and it's never been truer than it is at this minute. She knows what she's doing. Do you for one minute think that she'd be spending her money on that girl if she didn't expect to get it back with a good big interest? She's not bringing her up like a lady, educating her and giving her music and all that, just for the fun of it. No indeed! I knew the Aldens too well to ever suspect that one of them would throw away her money for mere pleasure."

"You don't mean — ?" Mrs. Mullin looked the question. She could not put it into words.

"That's just what I mean," laughed Kate. "You'll find that Debby Alden either knows or has some suspicion who that child is. It may be that her folks are well-to-do, and they'll pay Debby well when she lets them know of the child."

"Dear me! Who would have thought that Debby Alden would have been so far-sighted," she said. "No doubt, the child's folks are well off, and will pay Debby handsomely."

"Why, of course! Or why should she take all this trouble?" At this, Mary was about to come up with the change. Her father seized her hand. "You have it wrong," he cried. "Go back."

She returned to the cash drawer and deliberated long upon making the change. She knew not her father's purpose in sending her back. But having faith in his business ability, she obeyed without a word, and kept at the account until he let her know that he wished her to return. Meanwhile, Kate Bowerman, all unconscious of the little by-play which had been enacted before her eyes, continued her conversation with Mrs. Mullin.

"Debby forgot herself one day and let it slip that she knew more about the child's

mother than she had told any one. I remember where the ticket that the woman
had was from, and where she was going.
I've a sharp memory for such things. Some
day, when I've time, I mean to write to
those places and just find out. A woman
and child disappearing isn't something
that's going to be forgotten in fifteen
years."

"No, I guess not," said Mrs. Mullin.
At this she grew reminiscent, and repeated
in detail all the events of that day. But
the details were too clear in Kate's mind
to enjoy hearing another repeat them.

"Yes, I know all about it, Hattie, from
A to Z. But we've something else to
attend to now. Where is that girl with
my change? Is she never coming?"

At this Abner Stout raised his voice, and
admonished Mary not to be so slow. She
hurried forward with the change. Mrs.
Bowerman and her friend went on their
way. Abner Stout stood behind the counter

until late that night, his hands busy with scales and twine, but his mind weaving a great scheme by which gold might be added to his constantly increasing hoard.

CHAPTER IX

A T the hour appointed that afternoon, a merry party had gathered at Jane's home, preparatory to starting on the skating expedition. Hyner was a little village six miles distant. To skate there was no task at all. It was the return trip against the wind and the imperceptible slope of the ice-bed which tried the mettle of the skaters.

They were about to set forth when Mary Bowerman entered ready for the trip, her skates slung on a strap over her shoulders. She made no explanation in regard to her change of plans.

"I was afraid I would be late," she said, "and I walked so fast that I am out of breath."

The others waited until she had rested, and then started out. Mrs. Orr followed them to

the gate, admonishing them to be careful
and not to run any risks while skating.

"Don't worry, mother," said Ralph.
"The ice is as solid as a rock. I haven't
seen such ice as this for years. One could
skate anywhere on it."

"It is just that confidence that may
cause the trouble," she replied. "You may
be so sure that you will not take the trouble
to look about you and rush on into danger.
Do be careful, girls. Ralph, remember
they are under your care."

"I certainly will not forget. I'll take
care of them, mother." He looked quite
able to fulfil his self-appointed task. He
was in his third year in college, and had
won a reputation as an athlete. He was
big, broad-shouldered, and sinewy.

When they reached the ice, he called
out to those in advance: "Wait a moment,
girls, until I come. I'll put on your skates."

A merry laugh greeted him from Jane
and Hester.

"You would have a glorious task, Ralph," said Hester. "Twelve girls with skates to have put on. Why, the last one would be chilled to the marrow before her turn came."

"It will take but — " he began. He was already upon his knees with Jane's skates in his hand.

"We can manage very well, thank you, Ralph," said Janet. She had one skate on and the lever turned, and was strengthening her ankle with a heavy strap as she spoke. Mary Bowerman alone made no effort to put on her skates, but stood close by Jane, waiting until Ralph had finished tightening the levers.

"Put mine on, Ralph. I hate working with the cold steel, and the buckles always hurt my hands."

The other girls were ready. As they waited, they tested their skates, making fancy curves and figures upon the ice and circling about Ralph and Mary while he tightened the straps.

"Let me lead the way," he said, rising and drawing on his gloves. "I'll pick out a safe course. Mother is so afraid of air-holes. I honestly don't believe there is one for miles about. Nevertheless, I'll skate ahead." He looked about the group, uncertain who needed his help most.

"Will you skate singly or together? Who wants me to help them?"

"You'd better take Della," suggested Jane. "She hasn't skated as we have, and she'll tire sooner."

"Very well," he replied, holding out his hands to the frailest and youngest of the set. She smiled as she said: "I'm very glad. I do not skate well alone. I've always skated with one of my brothers, and I'm timid when alone."

"You should practise skating without help. I would not attempt it on a trip like this, but some afternoon when you have no definite place to make. It will make you more independent." Then he

added with a smile: "Skating is like everything else. You must go it alone, if you
do it well."

One cannot skate and talk, so the conversation stopped. Ralph and Della led
the way. Back of them in single file and
separated by several rods came the others
of the party. Jane, whose muscles were
accustomed to this form of exercise, was in
the lead. Back of her came Hester, while
Janet, panting and perspiring, was at the
rear. With long, sweeping strokes the line
swept down the river. Each movement
was graceful, and the rhythmical sway of
their bodies was as easy and graceful as
that of the sedges moved by the breeze.

Hyner was reached with no unusual
experiences. The girls were warm with
exercise.

"I feel fine except for my feet," said
Jane, as she tried to walk, "but they are
asleep."

"You would have your straps as tight

as I could draw them," said Ralph. "That is what caused the trouble."

She was not alone in her discomfort. Each girl, as she attempted to walk across the beach without her skates, stumbled awkwardly, and gave little shrieks as she struck a clump of earth or a rock.

"My feet feel as though they weighed ten pounds," said Della. "I can scarcely drag them along."

Each expressed her discomfort in a new and individual way, yet laughed between the twinges of pain.

"I'm glad we are here at last," said Jane, as they mounted the steps of the little country hotel. "I've been told that this place is only a hundred yards from the river. It seemed a mile while I was walking."

"A mile!" said Della, sinking into the chair she came to first. "I'm sure it was ten miles. My feet were so numb that I couldn't lift them, and so I struck every

rough place on the beach. I think there
was ten thousand of them, and every time
I struck one, a million little sharp pains
ran from my toes to the top of my head."

The girls laughed at the exaggeration.
Della was addicted to the use of such expressions. She knew no happy medium.

"I intend remembering that for rhetoric.
Our lesson for Monday is a review of figures
of speech. I'll use that for the hyper-
bole." This was from Janet. As she
spoke, she glanced toward Della. "Is that
the way the word is pronounced, Dell?"
she asked.

"Use your own taste in regard to it," responded Della, with a show of indifference.
"I shouldn't have called it that."

"I think not," replied Janet. Then,
turning to the others, she said: "You girls
were at the board and didn't hear Dell
recite. She said an exaggerated form of
expression was called a hyper-bowl."

"I'm glad I said it," said Della, good-naturedly. "Janet has enjoyed it so. She's told every one that she's met since."

They had drawn about the great stove which stood in the middle of the hotel parlor. Twilight had fallen, and the room was dusky. Ralph had gone to see what the prospects for supper were. The girls sat with their feet on the fender, chattering of school affairs as they awaited his return.

"I hope there'll be enough to eat," said Janet. "I'm as hungry as a bear."

"I'm as hungry as two bears," said Hester. "I hope the landlady will not think that we're a frail and delicate set. Let's appoint a committee to tell her how hungry we are."

"Better have Della as chairman," said Janet. "She'll use enough 'hyper-bowls' to convince the woman that a regiment has come down upon her."

"Are you as hungry as that?" said a pleasant voice, as the woman of the house entered. "Your supper will be ready soon, and I promise you that there will be enough of it. It is growing dark; I'll light the lamps."

She lighted the lamps and opened the piano. "Perhaps some of you would like to play," she said, as she left the room.

"I should like to," said Janet, " — but I can't."

Orpha, during all the chatter and light talk, sat silent. It was difficult to know whether she appreciated what was going on, or whether it was an enigma to her. The only part she took in the conversation was "Why?" or "Is that so?"

Supper was prepared for them in the course of half an hour. By this time they were able to step without shrieking with mingled pain and laughter. The landlady outdid herself in service, standing by the table and urging them to partake heartily of the fare.

"If you intend skating home, you'll need

to eat well, for there's a stiff breeze starting up, and you know how the wind on the river cuts."

Ralph excused himself from the table to investigate the condition of the weather. "Let's start back at once," he said, as he rejoined the girls. "There is a little wind. I suppose it will get stronger as the hour grows later. We'll start now and miss the worst."

Hurrying into their wraps and giving their feet a last warming at the fender, they made ready to depart. They found a stiff breeze sweeping along the river. With as little delay as possible, they were on their skates, battling against it. Ralph had gone ahead with Della and Janet on either side. Back of them came the others in single file, their heads bent forward and their skirts flying in the wind. They had skated some distance when Edith Rank, who led the line, paused to wait until the others came up.

"We'll skate easier if we go three by three," she said. "This wind takes one's strength. We'll find we'll not be so apt to flounder about with three. Come, girls!" She held out a hand toward Mary and Hester. The latter hesitated, but only for a moment. She did not wish to skate arm in arm with Mary, but a river of ice on a cold night, with the wind blowing, is not a pleasant place for the airing of grievances. Hester held out her hand, and she and Edith with Mary between started on.

Ralph and the others were ahead. The ice crackled under their feet. The trunks of trees along the shore cast weird, gaunt shadows. The three skated without speaking, having no surplus energy to give to conversation. With their heads bent down to protect their faces from the wind, they could not see far in advance. Unconscious of their course, they had moved nearer shore, just where Paddy's Run enters the river. There were eddies and ripples here, and the ice had formed with air-holes.

Suddenly, as the three skates lifted to take a long stroke, Mary gave a scream, let go her hold upon the girls, clutched wildly, and went through the ice. Hester lost no time in screaming.

"Skate for Ralph as fast as you can!" she said to Edith. The girl, understanding what was best to be done, bent her head to the wind and skated up the stream as fast as she was able. She watched her course now, and kept well over the deep water.

Ralph, with the two girls clinging to him, was not making great headway. Edith had made but a half mile before she reached him. "Go back! It's Mary!" she panted, catching to the girls to check her speed and steady herself. Without a word, Ralph turned and went back.

Hester had no sooner given Edith the word to hurry for Ralph, than she threw herself flat upon the ice, and, reaching forward, caught Mary under the arms. Thus supported there was no danger of Mary going under, although she was in up to her arms. She began to cry with fright.

"Ralph will be here in a minute," said Hester. "It's only an air-hole, — the ice is strong where I am. I will not let you go." Her words came brokenly, as supporting Mary's weight only for these few minutes had almost exhausted her, and the ice had chilled her limbs into numbness.

It was only a few minutes until Ralph was there. He threw himself flat upon the ice as Hester had done, and grasping Mary firmly, cried out: "All right, Hester, pull as hard as you can! Her dress is frozen fast."

He was big and strong enough to drag her out. "Keep her there just a minute," he said, putting Jane's arms about her. "Here, Hester," and he stood and lifted

her up. "You're all right, now," he said
encouragingly. "Edith, you and Jane skate
with Hester. I'll take Mary. Skate as
though the wolves were after you."

He had picked Mary up in his arms.

"See that light! We are within a half-
mile of Debby Alden's. Go for it."

He skated as fast as was possible with
Mary in his arms. The others kept in
advance of him.

When they reached the bank, he did not
wait to remove his skates, but with them
on cut his way over the ice and stones of
the beach.

"Don't take me in to Aldens', Ralph,"
cried Mary. "Debby Alden will not let
me stay. She'll put me out."

"Don't you believe it," he said. "She'll
put you to bed and dose you up until you
couldn't take cold if you tried."

"Take me any place but there."

Ralph laughed, and hurried through
the Alden garden to the house. He gave

He did not wait to remove his skates — *Page 184.*

little thought to Mary's request, believing
that she was so badly frightened that she
did not know what she was saying.

Debby Alden wasted no time in use-
less questions. After her quick, "Where's
Hester?" and Ralph's reply, "She's coming. The girls stopped long enough to
take off their skates," she said nothing,
but took Mary from Ralph's arms and
carried her into the kitchen.

"Sit there with your feet in the oven
while I make a bed ready for you." She
paid no attention to Mary's feeble words
of remonstrance. In a moment the kettle
was on the stove, the fire-brick heating
on the front griddle, while Debby Alden
was upstairs making up the bed with
extra blankets.

Mary's teeth were chattering when
Debby came back. The girls had crowded
into the kitchen. Hester, in spite of her
hard skating, was blue with the cold.
"Hurry upstairs and get into bed, Hessie.

I've double blankets on. Slip between them. Jane, run along and rub her feet after she's in. Edith, fill the water-bag when the kettle boils, and bring it upstairs. The others take off your wraps, and get warm. I'll see to Mary."

She took the shivering girl by the arm. "Hurry upstairs to the back bedroom. It's the warmest. There's two beds, and you and Hester can be company for each other."

Soon she had both girls in bed between blankets, with hot-water bottles and bricks about them. Edith had been sent downstairs to brew a pitcher of catnip tea. When danger of a chill was past, and the girls were snug and warm, Debby Alden went downstairs. The little group had gathered about the kitchen stove with their feet in the oven or on the fender.

"I'm going to give you a good hot cup of coffee and have you well warmed up, then I'm going to send you home. Your mothers will worry if you're late."

She brought forth the coffee urn and cups. "While I'm attending to the coffee, tell me how it happened."

A babel of voices arose. Their fear having gone, excitement took its place. By broken sentences, many exclamations and interruptions, Debby Alden learned that Hester had acted the part of a heroine.

"And there lay Hester, stretched out flat, with her hands holding Mary under her arms. Hester was stiff with cold, and her sleeves were frozen to the ice where the water trickled over. She could scarcely move, but I told her to skate home. I couldn't carry two and, anyway, moving was better for Hester," said Ralph.

"I think I should have stood there until doomsday," cried Edith. This was the first excitement she had shown. "I was stunned, I'm sure. I could not have moved, but Hester cried, 'Go for Ralph,' and threw herself right across the broken ice. I didn't wait. I went as fast as I

could. I forgot everything but catching
up to Ralph. I'll never be able to skate
so fast again."

"There really wasn't any danger," explained Ralph, "but Hester did not know
that. There wasn't danger for her, I mean,
but if she hadn't have held Mary above
water, she would have gone under. You
see, Miss Alden, the air-hole was about a
foot across. Mary came with all her weight
upon it. Of course, when she went through,
the thin ice, for the radius of a foot, went
with her, but it was solid where Hester
and I threw ourselves. It was fully six
inches thick. So Hester was in no danger."

Debby Alden pressed her lips grimly.
"If there had been danger, it would have
been all the same to Hester. To try to
save a companion was the only thing for
her to do — danger or no danger. Of
course, she acted quickly and without
thinking, but actions of that kind are more
apt to show of what sort folks are than

actions that come after thought and deliberation. I'm glad Hester showed the proper instincts."

She poured the coffee and passed it to her guests. "It may keep you awake, but it will keep you from being chilled."

When they had finished, she said: "Now, I'm going to send you home. It's long after ten o'clock, and your parents will be worried about you. Ralph, will you stop in at the Bowermans' and tell Kate that Mary will stay with Hester all night? You need say nothing of what has happened. Mary is comfortable now, and there's no danger of her taking cold. I've done all I could, and there's no use in Kate's running over here to-night and getting nervous and excited. We'll tell her about it in the morning."

"I presume, Miss Debby, that this will be the last time Hester will be allowed to go skating," said Jane.

Debby Alden shook her head in negation. "No, she may go just as she always has, when the ice is reasonably safe. I never wish her to take foolhardy risks, but neither do I want her kept in a band-box, wrapped up in cotton."

She came with them to the door, holding a lamp high in her hand to light them down the garden path.

"All right, Miss Debby. Good night," they called back. She responded warmly, and, turning back into the kitchen, closed the door upon the darkness and the ris-ing wind.

Upstairs the two girls lay in great feather-beds in the bedroom over the kitchen. They were warm; the danger of a chill, with all the ills which might follow in its wake, had passed. Yet they were not comfortable. At least, Mary Bowerman was not. She felt that an apology was due to Hester, or at least an expression of grati-tude for the effort Hester had made to save her. She was nervous and restless, in spite

of the copious draughts of catnip tea which
Miss Debby had given her.

She heard Ralph and the girls leave the
house, and their call of "good night" from
the garden gate. She could hear Hester
breathing, but could not tell whether she
were sleeping or awake. When she heard
Miss Debby coming upstairs, she closed
her eyes and pretended to be asleep. She
did not wish to talk with her now, and she
knew that Miss Debby would slip in to see
how her patients were getting along.

Debby put the lamp in the hallway,
turning it low that the light might not
waken the girls if they were sleeping. She
tiptoed in, in her stocking feet. Leaning
over Mary's bed, she laid her hand softly
upon her head and then upon her hand.
Both were warm and moist. With a sigh
of relief, she went to Hester.

"I'm all right, Aunt Debby," whispered
Hester. "I'm as warm as toast. I was
trying to stay awake until you came up.

Good night." She raised herself in bed and threw her arms about her aunt's neck. "Oh, Aunt Debby! when I saw Mary in the water to-night, I was sorry."

"Don't talk about it. There was really no danger," she replied brusquely. She understood what Hester was about to say. Sorry that she had kept warm in her heart her anger at Mary. "We'll not talk about it to-night, Hessie."

She kissed the girl, and went off to her own room. She had not wished Hester to express herself before Mary. "Mary Bowerman is the one who should feel sorry and ashamed," she said to herself.

Mary lay with her eyes closed, listening to Miss Debby moving about in her room. When the house had grown quiet and all danger of Miss Debby's hearing her had passed, she raised herself on her elbow and whispered, "Hester! Hester!"

There was no response. Hester heard, but her pride would not let her heed.

"Hester! why don't you answer? You are not asleep."

At this Hester raised herself on her elbow, and across the dimly lighted room the girls looked each other directly in the eyes.

"What is it?" asked Hester. She spoke calmly enough, although her heart was throbbing so violently that she could scarcely speak. She wished to be loved. Every friend was dear to her. She and Mary had played together since they were toddling babies. She liked Mary yet, in spite of all that had passed between them, and she was almost ready to forgive the insult and forget that Mary had proved herself false to truth and to friendship.

"You saved my life to-night. I suppose I'd be under the ice now, if you had not helped me up. I've been lying here a long time thinking about it. I wanted to tell you that I didn't tell you just what was true. Your mother was not really a common tramp. I shouldn't have said that. She had gone from her way and was walking into town."

So far, the attempt at confession and apology was good. Suddenly Mary paused. Perhaps the look of pleasure and relief which came to Hester's face was too much for Mary's malicious, selfish nature to bear. She laughed softly, and then added, "But the rest was true enough — the rest about no one knowing who you are, and Aunt Debby keeping you so you wouldn't be sent to the poorhouse."

For one instant Hester's frame stiffened. She was never slow about expressing herself when matters did not move to please her. Sharp, bitter words were upon her tongue, but she thought of her Aunt Debby, who must never know that she knew that she belonged nowhere, and that no one claimed her. She pressed her lips together, arranged her pillow with the greatest care, and lay back as though to sleep.

"I have a lot of things that I'd like to say to you, Mary Bowerman," she said in whispers, "but they'll not be said to-night."

CHAPTER X

ABNER STOUT'S mind was planning great things. When the store had closed, and the family gathered about the board, he was silent. Jane prepared her most savory dishes, which her brother-in-law ate without comment, and not so much as smacked his lips with satisfaction, as was his wont. By these signs his family knew that some great plan had presented itself to his mind, so they spoke in whispers when he was present, and gave him room at the table and when they sat about the fire.

A week passed before he lifted up his voice and spoke. It was after supper. Mary and Esther were in the parlor entertaining friends with music. Joel and John had dressed themselves with care, donned their finest overcoats, and with canes in hand went for a promenade in the public

thoroughfare. They were the only family
of their class in town. They had not the
privilege of calling upon young ladies at
their homes, so their social life was made up
of promenading upon the public square and
ogling every one who passed. Their clothes
were always redolent with perfume, and a
supercilious smirk was upon their lips.

So it was that Abner and his sister-in-law
sat by the fire alone. The room was in
shadows, the light having been turned low,
as the gas was metred. He was the promi-
nent, all-absorbing presence in the room.
Jane, worn, humble, and a dependent upon
his good graces, sat in the background upon
a rocking-chair, yet not rocking lest she
disturb the serenity of Abner's thoughts.
She was ingratiating and sycophantic. She
had fed upon the bread of charity all her
life, and her manner was apologetic for exist-
ing at all. Yet she was not naturally dull,
but independent thought and action had
long been crushed out of her. Her living

depended upon the favor of others, and to obtain that favor was the sole ambition left within her.

Suddenly Abner looked up at her; his sharp, keen eyes gleamed through narrow slits of eyelids. He rubbed his hands together as though to wash them; his smile, intended to be pleasing, was but sinister; his oily voice was ingratiating as he addressed his sister-in-law.

"I know what your mind is working on, Jane. You grieve too much about it, Jane."

She looked up quickly, unable to understand the new tone in his voice. She had never known him to be sympathetic or tender. As to grieving! She was anything but that. She scarcely knew what she was thinking about. She knew only that she was glad that she could sit all evening in quiet, for her back had grown weary with sorting rags from daylight until bedtime. She knew her brother-in-law well. He could be sympathetic and tender only when these qualities paved the way for his own purpose. She looked at him, but did not reply. She knew that something lay beyond his remark, and waited to hear.

"Poor 'Liza has been dead sixteen years now. It's never been the same with me since she went away. She was a fine woman — was 'Liza, my wife." He sniffled and rubbed his eyes with the back of his hand. Jane waited patiently as became a woman of her humble position. She offered no word of sympathy, for in spite of his attempt to wipe away the tears of grief, she knew that his eyes were dry. She had not heard him speak of 'Liza since the day she was buried from the East Side of New York, where she had died from fever contracted from sorting junk and rags which had been collected from an infected region of the tenements.

Her death had occurred eighteen years ago, and Abner had engrossed his time and

mind so in business that he had not mentioned her in all these years.

He heaved a prodigious sigh and continued: "You're sitting around dopish all
the time, and thinking of Eliza. You
grieve as though it was only yesterday she
died. You're always sniffling and feeling
bad." He gave her no opportunity to
reply, but continued: "You can't get over
her going away, taking little Ruth with her.
Every day you sit around and cry as though
your heart was broke. It's always, ' Abner,
I must go to 'Liza's grave. I want to
know that she's buried decently as a Chris-
tian should be. I hain't never happy when
I think that she's lying away from her
people, and no tombstone over her.' You
keep talking about her every day till I'm almost crazy listening to you. Hain't that the
way you've been acting right along, Jane?"

He glanced at her furtively. He had
been sitting with his face buried in his
hands, the very attitude of dejection and

grief. Now he glanced at her through his long, thin fingers, as though to study the effect of his words.

Her face was utterly devoid of expression. She rocked gently backward and forward. It was not yet clear to her mind toward what end he was working, so she discreetly did not commit herself to speech. But when he kept his sharp eyes upon her and repeated his query, "Isn't that the size of it, Jane?" she nodded her head in affirmation and replied, as she knew he wished her to do, "I guess it's that way if you say so, Abner."

Again he sniffled and wiped the imaginary tears from his eyes. "It is sixteen years next June since Ruth was born. My, but she was a fine child, with lots of hair curling about her head. She was dark like Mary — same eyes and hair." He paused a moment as though to let his thoughts dwell tenderly upon this child of his. The attempt at tears was forgotten. He spoke in

clear, incisive tones, which cut and rang
like his own silver dollars as they fell on
the counter. He was the business man
now, ready to sacrifice any one or every one
to his own interests.

Jane did not break the silence. She was
ignorant of his plans, so the most tactful,
the surest thing, was to maintain a discreet
silence. After a moment, he continued: —

"'Liza was never the same woman after
Ruth was born. Never seemed to get
through her work, and always fussing and
fretting. That was sixteen years ago since
Ruth was born. Hain't that about right,
Jane?"

Again she nodded in affirmation. All
this was new to her. She had heard of no
Ruth except that one who went gleaning
in the fields of Boaz. But if Abner had a
good and sufficient reason for wishing there
to be a Ruth who was born sixteen years
ago, she knew no reason to refuse him such
comfort. So far, she was wholly in the

dark as to his intentions, but an understanding of his plans could never be had
by asking questions. He would divulge as
much as he wished her to know, and the
time and place would be of his own choos-
ing. That she was necessary to the further-
ance of his plan was evident, else he would
have told her nothing.

He watched her covertly for a few
minutes. He wondered if she would be as
'Liza had often been — too dense to follow
his lead in business matters. Eliza with
her big, innocent eyes, tell-tale expression,
and hesitancy in agreeing with statements
which he had made, had ruined many a
sale for him. But Jane possessed one advantage over her sister. No one could tell
her thoughts or intentions from her face.
Even to him they were a closed book.

He studied her furtively from between
his fingers. Her face was as heavy and
as expressionless as a block of wood. It
seemed safe to continue.

"You've never been the same person since 'Liza went off. Of course, you felt badly. Didn't we all feel just that way, and didn't we do everything to find her? But it's no use of spoiling your whole life. After she went and I knew there wasn't the remotest chance of finding her, I put my mind on business. As I said then, I can never be a happy man, but I'll be successful. I owe that much to my children. I'll leave them a little to make life easier. There's just one thing about 'Liza going off and taking Ruth the way she did. I think she was sicker than we thought. I spoke sharp once or twice to her about not taking hold and helping about the shop, but somehow she didn't seem to have any spirit. I honestly think she wasn't just right in her head. If I'd realized at that time how miserable she was, I'd never mentioned shop, and had up a doctor and sent her off somewhere to get well; although I had but a few dollars, I'd spent my last cent to have had her well, but I didn't know. I didn't realize. I was all wrapped up in trying to make a little so she and the children could live in comfort."

This new story of her sister's life was like a romance to Jane. So far as outward show was concerned, she listened with patience; but inwardly she was wondering as to the reason for the new version, and speculating as to the outcome.

His sharp gray eyes gleamed in the darkness. He was so much the actor that for the time he almost believed the story he was constructing.

"She's dead — I feel that she is dead," he said at last, in his sharp, metallic tone. "Surely, if she was living, she would have sent word. If not to me, at least to you, Jane, or to her children. But there's never been the scratch of a pen — not a scratch except that little note that she left pinned to a curtain, for all the world like a stage woman. That was one other thing that

made me think that Eliza wasn't just herself. She was never no hand for such
stagey games — running off and leaving a
note behind her. She was a woman with
good horse sense, and kept to her work
and said little. I have that letter yet, —
scratched on brown wrapping paper, — a bit
she tore from a package. It hain't writ
plain, for she was never nothing of a
scholar."

He had told Jane enough to set her
thinking. That was quite enough for one
evening. He was like a skilful fisherman,
who does not immediately attempt to draw
in his heaviest catch. He had her on the
hook. He knew that tact and skill would
be required to "land" her.

For a week the name of Eliza was not
mentioned in the family. Jane, knowing
her people well, knew that this silence be-
tokened neither lack of interest nor change
of plans. If Abner thought it wise to be
silent, well and good. She could keep her

lips as close as others. While she prepared
the savory stews, washed dishes, and cleaned
up the kitchen floor, she did much thinking.

Meantime, Abner, as he smacked his lips
over the palatable dishes, complimented her
highly upon her frugality and the delightful
results achieved without a great expenditure.

"Extravagance! Extravagance!" he exclaimed one day, as he rolled his eyes
heavenward and clasped his hands together. "It is the curse of our country.
Merchants want to live like kings, and
beggars like merchants. You mustn't be
extravagant, Jane. Save the scraps, for I
have so little, Jane, so little."

Jane kept her own counsel. Abner was
not generally free with compliments, yet, as
the week passed, at every meal he beamed
upon her and commended her for her
frugality.

"When your work is finished, Jane, come
into the store," he said one day. "You
are 'Liza's sister, and always stood by her

when she needed a friend, and I mean to show you that Abner Stout is not one to forget a kindness to him or his. So come in and pick a dress for yourself — trimmings, linings, and all." He set his thin lips close. His features were keen and sharp, at variance with the generosity expressed by his words. He turned to his eldest son, who was his likeness in looks and business methods. "When your Aunt Jane comes in, I want you to show her what there is in black goods. Let her have something fine and good. You have alpaca, haven't you? The kind that retails at fifty cents?"

Jane accepted the gift without comment. She was humble, dependent. It was not her place to pick and choose and declare her desire like those who had money in the business. This life was fine, compared to that with her brother's family. She knew no reason to complain.

Abner attended strictly to business while in the store. But at hours during the day when business was dull, he encouraged his customers to linger and talk with him. On these occasions he had little to say beyond a question now and then. But he was an excellent listener, and many of his customers, particularly those women who lived on isolated farms and drove to town but once a week, found him interesting company. He encouraged them to speak of their lives, incidents that had happened in this little valley. Wholly unconscious that he had a subtle purpose in leading them to talk, they told all they knew of their own history and their neighbors'. So he learned in detail all that had occurred in the valley for a score of years past. He knew of the accident which had occurred at the crossing. He could have described, had he been asked, each detail of her feature and dress. He knew the reputed age of the child this woman had carried in her arms. It was not until he was quite sure of all that could be known concerning Hester Alden's life and parentage that he spoke again to his sister-in-law.

"What a beautiful child our little Ruth was," he began suddenly, as they sat by the kitchen stove with the gas turned low, for it was sold by the meter. Jane was rocking slowly but steadily. She did not glance at the speaker or suggest in any way that she had heard him.

"She would have been just sixteen years old last June," he continued. "She favored Mary more than any other member of the family. Every one who saw her spoke about her big dark eyes and long lashes. Dark hair in soft rings about her head. Hain't that about right, Jane? Wasn't Ruth just such a looking child when her mother ran off with her and started to go to Chicago?"

Jane looked steadily into his eyes.

"I guess she must have looked that way," she said wearily.

"Guess? I should think you would know. If you have grown so dull that you've forgotten how your own sister's child looked, you'd better go back and live with Reuben. It will be too hard for you here — the work and all. Ruth was just such a looking child as I said; plump, with black hair in curls. Hain't I right? You seem afraid to speak out."

"Yes; that's how she looked. I remember now."

"Do you remember how I felt over Eliza's going off in that way and taking our baby? I couldn't stand the place. I sold out, sacrificed everything, and left the place. I never felt like settling anywhere till I came here. Then it seems as though I was satisfied. I've said time and again that somehow I had a feeling that I was near my little Ruth. That was the way I talked right along. Wasn't it?"

He looked keenly at her. His sharp gray eyes seemed to look deep into her heart. He had the power of making her agree to any statement which he might choose to make.

"Yes, indeed. You've said them very words time and time again," she responded.

He waited a moment, looking at his companion to see if she were grasping the import of his speech, and seeing that she was, he continued: "It's just sixteen years the fourth day of next June, Jane, since 'Liza took Ruth and went off. Remember that, Jane? You're getting old, and although your memory's good, it hain't quite what it was. I shouldn't like it at all if folks would say that you had forgotten your sister. Her loss was more to be remembered than though she had died in her bed, like a decent woman is supposed to die."

Jane nodded. She was beginning to see a glimmer of light in regard to this new story of her sister's life. Abner was satisfied with her quiet acquiescence. It pleased him more than any words could have done.

When he felt that she was responding in the proper spirit, and that in her he would find a reliable if not an energetic helper,

he continued his monologue. He dwelt at
length on the causes which led his wife
to become dissatisfied with her home. He
attributed the dissatisfaction to the condition of her nerves rather than to any material thing. He reproached himself for
having spoken sharply to her, and in the
same sentence excused himself for the act,
by declaring that he had not realized how
miserable in health she had been.

So admirably did he act the part that for
the time he believed the story he was re-
lating. His thin lips pressed together in
their cruel, grasping selfishness; his keen
little gray eyes looked furtively upon his
companion as he watched the effect of his
words upon her.

He told how he had slaved to provide
for her and the children. How but a few
weeks before her disappearance he had
purchased for her a handsome black skirt,
and fine shirt-waist of white madras.

He grew quite eloquent, and went into

details concerning these garments. He described the cut and length of the skirt, and the width of the flounce which adorned it. He described the quality of the goods so fully that Jane could have been able to select its counterpart from a score of black materials. He went so far as to mention the size and quality of the buttons which fastened the waist.

Jane nodded slowly, her head keeping time with the motion of her rockers. He continued his story, describing his long-lost wife as Jane did not at all remember her; for Eliza and she had greatly resembled each other. They had always been bony, sharp-featured girls, and had developed into scrawny, angular women, with little sharp eyes, straight thin noses, and sallow skins. The Eliza which Abner described to her was as unlike as possible to the Eliza which she had called sister. But Abner would not speak this without reason, and it was becoming and well for her, a humble dependent upon his charity, to agree to what he thought wise to say. When he had finished a description of this new Eliza, he added: "We know only that her ticket was on this road. We know nothing more than that. We never heard a word, though she said she'd write — that is, her letter on the scrap of brown paper said she'd write when she reached Chicago."

He sighed. Jane had listened so attentively, and her mind had become so engrossed in this subject about which she had thought for weeks, that she also sighed, and, with real tears in her eyes, murmured brokenly: "My poor sister! Poor 'Liza!"

Abner looked upon her with approval. He did not give her credit for genuine feeling, but was pleased with what he thought was her good acting. His spirits rose. He chuckled gleefully, and his eyes scintillated like bits of glass under the rays of a hot sun.

"I know how you've missed Eliza.

You're not one to talk much, but you've got a good heart in you, and you and Eliza thought a heap of each other. I'm pretty much the same way myself — not much for words, but pretty deep on feelings. If any of the folks should speak to you, you tell them how broke up I've been — never got over my great loss. That all I live for is the hope that I'll find my little girl. You speak up in that way, Jane, if folks should bring the matter up, you know." He looked sharply at her.

She nodded. "It won't be a word different than what you say," she said.

"Well, you've heard how I said it," was the rejoinder. Again she nodded. They understood each other. There was no need for further speech.

There was silence for some time. Abner Stout's shoulders bent forward until they were bow-shaped. He propped his head on his upturned hands, and his keen eyes pierced the semi-darkness of the kitchen.

Then he began again in his softest, most sycophantic tone.

"I never ask one to take me on my word alone. That hain't business. I exact pledges and proofs, and I do for others as much as I expect them to do for me. But here's you with your word. Your word's as good any time as the words of another. There's Herman Loeb, the money-lender, and there's William Shearer, both well-known. They'll remember Eliza, how she looked, and what she wore that day she took Ruth and left home. Herman has a great head for dates. He'll know the time to the hour."

Jane pressed her thin lips together, folded her arms across her bony chest, and rocked slowly for several minutes before she spoke. "I'd make sure, I'd make quite sure about him remembering, Abner. Folks will forget."

"He'll remember. Don't lose sleep on that, Jane. I'm sending Joel off to New

York this very night to see that Herman remembers. Eh? Joel?" He turned to address his eldest son who had that moment entered the room in an overcoat, and hat in hand. He wasted no energy in words. He understood the situation fully. He was to go to New York to see to it that Herman Loeb and the man Shearer remembered his mother, and the details of her disappearance as Joel would describe them, and also to bring to the minds of the two gentlemen certain little discrepancies of their own which were yet clear in the mind of Abner Stout.

Joel took a late train for the city. Abner instructed his daughters if customers should inquire for Joel, to say he was laid up with neuralgia. He knew no reason for the public knowing that Joel was in New York on business.

The next day Debby Alden came into the store. Abner himself hastened to wait upon her. She attended strictly to her purchasing with as few words as possible. The shopkeeper looked upon her with admiration, and when she departed his eyes followed her. To think of her, a woman, having foresight sufficient for such work; and ability enough to keep the secret to herself for sixteen years! What a wonderful creature she was! He would like to know her better. He might learn from her, and what wonderful results they might accomplish if they might work together for the same end!

CHAPTER XI

DEBBY ALDEN was much concerned about Hester's future in the high school. She suspected that Mary Bowerman had taunted her as being a child who had been reared on the charity of strangers, and what Mary had done became a possibility with every other pupil. Debby saw clearly that the following three or four years would be critical ones for Hester's peace of mind. Until this time the girls who were friends were but children, without a thought of a moment beyond the present, and with no knowledge of certain phases of life. Now they had come to the place where, with their half-knowledge, came self-assertion and self-confidence. They were willing now to blurt out what, in the course of several years, they would consider well before repeating.

As children they had been too innocent
to tell Hester that she by rights belonged
at the county home, and as women they
would have been too self-respecting, too con-
siderate of others, not to have kept such
knowledge to themselves. It was the years
between, when they were neither women
nor children, that Debby Alden dreaded.
It was now the first of March. School
would close the first week in June. Debby
felt that it would be better for Hester to
complete the freshman year, and that would
give her time enough to consider what was
best to be done before the opening of another term.

Miss Richards, who spent her winters in
the South, had not yet returned. She had
always been a help to Debby, and her suggestions in regard to Hester had been in-
valuable. Debby gave Miss Richards credit
for much that was fine in the girl.

The winter had passed quickly for both
aunt and niece. The freshman class had

taken the preliminary Latin, and were deep
in the translation of Cæsar. This work
had been extremely difficult for Debby, but
she clung to it with a tenacity of purpose
which had been a characteristic mark of
the Aldens for generations. Had the work
been easy, she might have laid it aside
without any pricks of conscience; but with
conditions as they were, it looked too much
to her like being conquered by a few pages
of printed matter. Her tenacity of purpose and faithfulness exerted an influence
over Hester. Debby realized this, and for
Hester's sake never grew faint-hearted,
whatever the task before her.

Hester's mind was quicker than hers,
especially along the line of literature and
language, as these never had been Debby's
strong points. She might have been a
mathematician, for she was logical, far-
sighted, and judicious. In order that she
could keep step with her niece, she purchased her own set of books, and put in

every spare moment that the housework
and sewing did not claim. Her sense of
humor never failed her. She often smiled
grimly as she sat alone translating the
Latin. A dozen years before had any one
told her that she would do just the thing
she was doing now, she would have put his
assertion by as not worth considering.
Looking back upon what she had accomplished during these years was a never-
failing source of delight to her. Her mind
had developed and broadened in a way she
would not have believed possible. Her
social life had become something worthy of
the name. She had, through Miss Richards's
introduction, become a member of a reading club. For several years she had met
and mingled with a conservative, cultivated
set of women who were friends of Miss
Richards.

Debby had never been at a disadvantage.
From the first she had been one with them;
for she had within her all the essentials of

high-breeding, and a high ideal of honor.
The thought of a lie appalled her; an im-
pure thought had never entered her mind
nor a coarse word crossed her lips. Although at first she was ignorant of the
niceties of manners which marked the
polished women she had met, yet they
recognized that she had within her that
which was the mark of nobility, and greater
than all the surface culture that the world
could give.

She had gone back to her forgotten
music since Hester was old enough to wish
to sing. She had taught herself much
about dainty needlework since that day she
had made Hester's first white dress. With
Hester in school and her friends coming in
for visits and calls, Debby had had young
life about her. This company meant extra
work and extra steps for the home-maker,
but it bore with it its own compensation,
as it kept her in touch with that "world
of buoyant spirits to whom the world was

green; with every goose a swan, and with
every lass a queen."

It was Debby Alden who took charge of
them when the sleighing parties were made
up, and who chaperoned the moonlight
walks and corn roasts. Before she knew
what had happened, her spirits were as
light and girlish as Hester's, while her
judgment and ideals had not lowered their
standard.

"She has done wonders for Hester," was
the common expression among the people
of the country-side. Debby heard and at
first accepted it without reservation. But
lately she had added to this judgment of
the people, "I have done some things for
her, but think what she has done for me!"

While awaiting Miss Richards's return,
Debby took inventory of her financial condition. The Aldens had ever been thrifty
folk, who would have gone in calico all
their lives rather than to exceed their income by so much as a penny. Indeed, they

had laid a little aside each year for the "rainy day." So it was that Debby, in addition to the farm, had been left a sum well invested. With the exception of the yard and her own little garden, the place had been hired out. The income from this had been sufficient to supply Hester and herself with their necessities. So far, they had had no longing for luxuries. Debby had never lived up to the full amount of her interest money.

When she considered Hester's future, she gave forth an expression of thankfulness that she had not been slack with her money. She believed that she would have enough, without touching the original principal, to send Hester to school for two years. She herself would live on very little while Hester was away. But at this point of thinking her courage always failed her. She could not think of what the house would be without Hester.

"Fifteen years, and she with me every

day of that time! Well, one can get in the habit of things in fifteen years."

Debby Alden had done that. In fifteen years she had lived only for Hester, and looked forward to the hour of her coming from school. Every act which she performed, every thought that came to her, had Hester as the centre about which they revolved. There had been a time when Debby Alden had hoped that Hester's relatives would find and claim her. Now she feared such a thing, and hugged to her heart the comforting thought that the laws of the land had made the child hers, and the love between them had grown so strong that unknown relatives, however near of kin, could never come between.

When Miss Richards returned from the South, Debby Alden at once called upon her.

"I'm troubled about Hester," she said.

"Isn't she well and happy? From your letters I judged she was both."

"She is just now, but I dread the future."

Then she told what had occurred during the winter. She did not mention Mary Bowerman's name. Nothing could be gained by making known to Miss Richards that young person's shortcomings, and Debby Alden was not one who traduced for the mere satisfaction of repeating ill of those whom she called neighbor.

"That has happened once, Eva," she said. "My little girl is proud; as proud as she can be of those things which a girl should be proud of. That is, of her good name, and her freedom from obligations, and then to be told that the name isn't hers, and that she's under great obligations to those who are not even kin! I tell you, Eva, it cut her deep. She never told me a word, but I could see how she was hurt."

"It never happened before, Debby, and it may never again. I think you worry needlessly."

But Debby Alden, as far as outside

practical affairs were concerned, was more far-sighted than Miss Richards.

"I think it will, Eva. I think it will occur more times in the next two years than it has or will again."

"Your reasoning may be logical, Debby; but it is beyond my comprehension. I feel as you do concerning Hester. I would not have her hurt in that way. There is no reason why she should bear the taunts of some malicious, ill-bred person." These were strong adjectives for Miss Richards. She observed her companion's look of surprise. "I am not speaking without thought, Debby. I mean what I say. No one but a malicious, ill-bred person would speak tauntingly of such matters to the person who is most interested. Hester should be spared a recurrence of such an experience. But I believe it will not come to her again."

There was always peace and calm in Miss Richards's presence. No phase or condition held fear or terror to her. She

performed graciously those duties which
lay near at hand, and her energy never
expended itself in anticipating the difficulties of the future. She knew no social
standing. The woof and warp of her friendship was formed upon her moral worth.
She visited as gladly at the three-room
cottage as she did at the mansion. Neither
did she make distinctions of years. Her
friends were among old ladies and women
of mature years. Hester enjoyed a visit
with Miss Richards as much as Debby did,
and once, without considering the force of
her speech, she remarked after a day with
Miss Richards, "Well, Miss Eva is a Chris-
tian who is working hard at the business."

Now she was conscientious in her efforts
to see Hester's position from the same
point of view that Debby was seeing it.
She did not wish by so much as a word to
make it possible for Hester to be hurt
again in the same way.

"I think you are worrying needlessly,

Debby," she continued, after a moment's consideration. "For this reason. Among all the girls with whom Hester is intimately acquainted, but one may be so maliciously inclined. I know that Jane and Edith and Janet would suffer to the limit rather than do such a thing. Perhaps in all that set of girls one only lacks self-control and breeding. Hester has learned who that is. Will she not keep from her? I think, Debby, that Hester will never again put herself in a position for that girl to speak to her so."

"You haven't been with girls as much as I have, Eva. I remember grandmother Palmer used to talk about young people climbing fools' hill. I thought then it was merely an old lady's saying, but I must confess now that I believe there is a good bit of philosophy in those old saws."

"Perhaps a grain of wheat in a bushel of chaff, Debby. Much husk and little meat."

"In some old sayings, perhaps. But I'm learning that this has more than one grain of wheat in it. You see it's this way, Eva. The greater number of the girls have been well reared. But up to this time they've been disciplined at home, and have had no responsibility, no choice in their line of conduct, which was right and proper, for no child has judgment enough to know what is best to do or be left undone. They have been children all these years. But now they've reached the place where they've begun to think and act for themselves, and their law of judgment and reason begins to show. They'll do silly, reckless things now, that they'll be ashamed of in three or four years. They're not babies, to have reason spanked into them, and they're not old enough to be talked to as one talks to women. It's these two or three years on fools' hill that I'm dreading for Hester."

"Yes, I understand, Debby. Have you

thought of any plans? Have you anything in view?"

"I have thought a great deal, but I waited until you had come back before I'd made up my mind to anything. She must go to school. I stopped when I was sixteen; but schools were not what they are now, and I intend that Hester shall be educated. I thought of several places, — boarding-schools, I mean, — but I haven't decided. There's Arlington, and Exeter, and a school where some of Jane Orr's friends went. Petrikin Hall, I think, is the name."

"Yes, I've had several young friends who went there. It is excellent in many ways. What do you wish most of all, Debby?"

Debby Alden considered well before replying. It was difficult to put into words what she wished for Hester.

"I wish her to know a good deal about books, but I don't wish her to get the idea that they are the best and only things in

the world. I wish her to take them as
incidentals in life, not as the chief end to
be attained." She looked up quickly at
her companion. Miss Richards could not
restrain a smile at Debby's terseness. "I
understand what you mean, Debby. What
else?"

"I wish a school where she will be taught
that high ideals and doing one's duty are
worth more than brains. Now I admire
bright people, Eva. I'm not wishing to
detract one iota from those who have great
brain power. But I hold that there's something greater. When I study the people
who were brought up here, whom I've
known since I was a toddler, I've found that
it isn't always the smart, brainy ones who
have accomplished the most good. I wish
Hester to know about books and to be
trained how to use them. But I wish her
to be taught to be honest and honorable,
to do her share of work wherever she is, and
I wish her to have her own ideas about

things, and not to do so and so because
Jane Brown or Jane Smith or some one else
has done it."

"I think Petrikin Hall is such a place.
What a student *is* counts there for more
than what she has. They pay a great deal
of attention to manners, though. Girls
are trained in many of the nice little ways
observed in cultivated society."

"I wish Hester to be well-mannered.
I've always wished her to be like you, Eva.
I should be satisfied if she'd be another
Miss Richards."

"I hope she will be a better, stronger
woman than I have been," was the reply.
"But I have not wanted in the effort,
Debby. I think I have made of Eva Richards as much as Eva Richards could be.
But Hester is stronger both physically
and mentally than I have been. She has
a strength of will which I lacked." She
hesitated just a moment, and then looking
into her friend's face continued, "You'll

understand me, Debby, I think, that Hester must belong to good people. You have trained her well, I know. But all the training in the world would not eradicate the traces of a low and weak people. Blood will tell, and Hester shows that her people were honest and upright."

Her words, in place of pleasing Debby Alden, depressed her greatly. She was no longer worried, but distressed. She herself firmly believed that ancestry spoke in the descendants. But with what she believed she knew of Hester's people, she was ready to combat such an idea. "Nonsense, Eva. Give a child training, and you can make what you wish of it. You can take a puny, dwarf plant and develop it into a giant of its kind. Why not with children?"

"But, Debby, you cannot cultivate a thistle until it becomes a rose, nor can you convert a sour apple into a sweet one. I should think you would be glad to believe such a theory, for with Hester the kind of

a girl she is, you might take it for granted
that her people were the best in the land.
But let us return to the school question.
Is there any particular line of work you
wish Hester to take up?"

"I had not thought so far. I have been
looking at the money side of the question
first. I can let her finish at some good
school without denying myself too much.
After that will be time enough for her to
consider work of any kind. She must
learn something, Eva, by which she can
provide for herself. As long as I am with
her there will be enough for us both, but
the greater part of my income dies with
me, and what is left will not be all that
Hester needs. So I intend that she shall
learn something that will keep her happy
and contented, and at the same time in-
crease her income."

Debby Alden was one who considered
the future from a practical standpoint.
Yet she was not one given to worry and

dim forebodings. She did take thought
for the morrow, but not worrying, distract-
ing thought.

"I've been perplexed about what work
to have her undertake. As yet she has
shown no particular inclination toward anything. Not that she is idle. She is never
that. She helps me with the housework,
and does her share, and she is speedy about
it, but I mean that she showed no inclination toward a profession, or life-work.
But, of course, she's young yet."

"Perhaps housework and home-making
may be her life-work. She may have a
home of her own, Debby. Indeed, I
think it is very possible, for Hester is surely
an attractive and lovable girl. And if she
made a very happy home, she could find no
nobler profession."

"I don't doubt that, but it's not to be
for Hester. I shall never allow Hester to
marry. She must never be allowed to get
that idea in her head."

"Why, Debby! I am surprised. Of course you love Hester, and we do not wonder at that. It is natural that you should wish to keep her with you, but you may not always be with her. You should think of her loneliness when you are gone. Isn't it a wee bit selfish, Debby, not to wish her to have a home of her own?"

"It isn't selfish. It's anything but that. But Hester must live as you and I have lived. It hasn't been a lonely life for me. The days are all too short, and even if it should be lonely, there's to be no choice for Hester. She must be Miss Hester Alden to the very last of her days."

Miss Richards shook her head. "I do not understand you to-day, Debby. You do not seem like yourself. You have strange notions, but Hester is a little girl yet, and the time for such questions is a long way off."

"But the proper time to settle some questions is before they ever come up.

Never by any word must Hester be given
such ideas. If she should talk to you on
such matters, — I know the young girls
come to you with half their worries, — I
wish you to discourage her. Don't countenance any idea of sentiment that may
come to her."

"Very well, Debby, if you think best.
Hester belongs to you, and you are the
one to decide as to her training. I shall
not allow her to talk to me on some subjects.
I do that out of respect to your wishes,
Debby, yet I do not agree with you. I
would not think too much about Hester's
future. We can make preparations and
do our planning, yet her life is beyond our
control. A greater power will put to
naught our work. Plan for Hester's school,
and forget other matters. They may
never be for you or me to decide."

Debby Alden leaned her head wearily
back upon the back of the chair. She closed
her eyes, and for a time sat without speak-

ing. By nature she was frank and open.
The Aldens had never been secretive.
There had been nothing in their lives
which would have caused them to blush
had it been heralded to the world. To
know that which a friend could not know,
to feel that there was one thing that she
had not told because of shame and fear,
had hung over Debby Alden for fifteen
years. When she thought of what she
was concealing, she felt like a criminal.
Her keeping this secret and rearing Hester
under false pretence was bearing with it
its own compensation. Her friends would
misunderstand and misjudge her as Eva
Richards was doing now; and as time
passed, and she of necessity must train
Hester as she knew it must be, she would
be yet more misunderstood and reproached.

For the first time she longed to ease her
conscience of its burden and rest it upon
some one else, if but for a moment. She
looked up at her friend. Her lips quivered

and her eyes filled with tears, but she forced them back. "I've been wanting to tell you something, Eva," she said, "something I've known for fifteen years, since the very day that Hester's mother came to my home and asked to rest. I've kept it a secret for Hester's sake. I know enough of the child's parentage — more than any one has ever suspected I know — to feel that I would commit a crime should I allow her to marry one whom I or my friends could receive into their homes. It is not selfishness in me; I wish to protect and guard my little girl. I cannot explain. I've carried the secret for fifteen years, and must carry it all the rest of my life."

"Very well, Debby. It is not my place to judge what you have done. Yet I would not anticipate the future. You will do as you have always done, perform each duty faithfully and cheerfully. You can do no more. Perhaps it is well. For Hester's life may be ordered on higher,

broader lines than it is given to us to con-
template.''

She laid her hand upon Debby's bowed
head. There was silence for a moment.
Then Miss Richards, with a sprightly, viva-
cious manner, began to talk of other matters.
So the subject of Hester's family was closed
between them, and never reopened.

CHAPTER XII

THE accident which occurred during the returning skate from Hyner was only an incident in the lives of the young people. They had been brought up by the water, and, although they realized its dangers, they also enjoyed hugely the recreation and sport which it afforded them. The experience caused them to be more watchful, but it did not cause one to be fearful enough to keep from the ice.

The winter was long and severe. The skating lasted until the last of March. Along the river, as far as the eye could carry, the ice swarmed with skaters. At night bonfires were built alongshore, torches were carried, and the sport continued.

The girls came home tired but happy. Their muscles grew strong and flexible, and the rhythm and motion of skating movements gave a new grace and ease to them.

One Saturday morning, several days after
Joel Stout had returned from New York,
where he had gone to tell Herman Loeb
and Will Shearer what they were to remember, Hester and her friends started
out for the river. The ice directly opposite the Alden home had been in constant use, and was so cut up that it was
impossible to longer skate on it. On this
account, the girls went to the river near the
west end of the town, where the ice had
been little used.

During the walk through town, Janet
had been fussing and grumbling about the
condition of the front levers. They had
not been at all satisfactory, and had tripped
her several times the previous evening.

"Your soles are not heavy enough,"
said Mary Bowerman, giving a quick sidewise glance at Janet's slender, shapely foot.
"It's perfectly silly trying to skate in shoes
several sizes too small."

Janet laughed. Mary's sharp remarks merely amused her. She replied to her lightly. "But what can I do? They are the very broadest my Cinderella feet can wear."

"My front levers wouldn't close tight enough either," said Jane. "I screwed them as tight as I could. I told Ralphie, and he cut off part of the screw. It took him almost an hour, but my skates fit nicely now. If you would tell him —"

"I will, Jane. I'd give a farm to have a pair fit as they should. But Ralph's changing them to-night will not make them fit this morning. Why, last night, every time I'd try to take a long glide and lift my foot, there would be my skate dangling from the heel strap. The toe-lever wouldn't hold at all. The only way I could skate was to take little, mincing steps, and not lift my foot."

"Use a strap across the toe," said Hester. "I have several good ones at home. If I'd thought, I'd have brought them."

Janet sighed, and then looked up at them with woe pictured upon her face. "You are surely the most sympathizing people. There have been two suggestions for making those miserable skates"—she shook them fiercely — "stay on, but neither plan is working just at present. I've made up my mind to go skating and do some of that fancy rolling. I think it looks fine, and I'll do it if I'm compelled to strap my skates on my hand."

"You can buy straps," said Edith. "If they'll make the matter right, why not stop in the store and buy two short ones? They'll not cost more than ten cents apiece."

Janet stopped and looked at the speaker.

"Edith Rank," she said with mock gravity, "do you realize that your suggestion is far worse than either of the others? It can't be carried out. Besides that, it makes me acknowledge my financial condition in the world. I haven't a penny with me. How can I buy two straps even at the ridiculously low rate of ten cents each?"

Janet was always looked upon as the humorous girl of the crowd. Such was her reputation, and her slightest remark was accepted as funny, and called forth either smiles or laughter. The girls laughed now. Janet looked annoyed.

"It's true," she exclaimed. "I am financially embarrassed — I haven't a penny with me, and allowance day is a week distant."

"Then allow me," said Hester, presenting her purse. "Help yourself, Janet. But I'm sure you'll not find more than fifty cents in it."

Janet did not hesitate to accept the offer.

"How good you are, Hester. You've made me happy for the morning, provided I can get the straps at Stout's, and they work as you say they will. Come, let us turn down Fourth Street, and the store will be right on our way. We can get on the ice from Fourth as well as Fifth Street."

As usual, Abner Stout's clerks were busy. The girls made their way to the department where the straps would likely be. Hester and Janet were in advance. Abner was waiting upon a customer when the girls came in. The moment his glance rested upon them, he turned and spoke in an undertone to his daughter Mary.

The girl made no response. She did not raise her eyes toward the group of girls by the counter, but silently and quickly left the store and went in the direction of the kitchen.

She was gone but a few moments when Jane stuck her head through the doorway, glanced about her, and then, coming up to her brother-in-law, said plaintively, —

"Abner, hain't you cut me off that cheese yet?"

Abner was slow to answer, so Jane walked across the room to the front of the counter.

This brought her face to face with Hester. She gave a sudden cry, threw her apron over her face, and began swaying her body to and fro as though overcome by sudden and intense grief. The attention of customers and clerks was attracted to her. Hester and Jane drew back, uncertain what to do. The people who were buying in the front of the store hurried back to know the cause of the trouble.

Jane swayed back and forth, her face hidden by the blue-checked gingham apron, and all the while she gave a peculiar cry of distress.

"What is ever the matter with the woman?" cried Abner in well-feigned alarm, as he hurriedly came from behind the counter. "I never knew her to carry on so. She's quiet and peaceful, Jane is."

He laid his hand upon her shoulder. "Jane, look here! What's the trouble with you? What ails you? You act as though you were crazy. Go on in the

house, and don't raise such a fuss. Mary
can take care of you if you are ill."

He had one hand on her shoulder, and
with the other he drew away the apron
from her face. She shrieked, and her body
shook with sobs, but the eyes which she
raised to meet Abner Stout's glance were
quite dry.

"What's ailin' you, Jane?" he repeated.
"What do you mean by scaring customers
into fits until they shake as though they
had the ague? If you're sick, go back into
the house, and Mary will see to you."

At this Jane yelled and shrieked louder
than before.

"Ails me? What's been ailin' you
right along? What's been the matter with
your eyes? You've all been blind as bats.
Can't you see Eliza's child? She looks
just like Eliza when we used to play together — before you ever met her, Abner."

She raised herself and pointed to the
girls, who, absorbed in what was going on,

were wholly unconscious of their own conspicuous position, quite at the front of the
crowd of shoppers.

At these words Abner raised his eyes
and looked at the girls. He gave a hasty
glance, and then, leaning forward, stared
at Hester.

"Land of love!" he cried. "Jane, I
believe you're right. Never was there such
a likeness. It's Eliza herself come back
to me." Then he pressed his thin lips
together, clasped his hands as though with
a mighty effort he was controlling himself, and all the while kept his eyes upon
Hester as if he could not remove them.

Customers came in, and, attracted by the
cries and the crowd, pushed forward. The
main aisle of the store was jammed. Hester
and Jane looked about them, eager to escape. But behind them was a crowd of
people so closely packed in that a passage
among them would have been impossible,
while before them stood the figures of the

old man and his sister-in-law, swaying
their bodies and gazing upon Hester as
though she had hypnotized them.

Janet's mind was upon her skating.
She was growing impatient of this delay.
She looked about her, hoping to find some
means of escape, but every thoroughfare
was closed. She sighed and turned to
Hester with the remark, "Oh, had I the
wings of a dove!" She looked over the
heads of the people as though selecting a
course to follow, should her wish come true.
The remark was so like Janet. Hester
laughed aloud. At this Jane Farwell gave
forth a louder shriek. "Did you see that
smile — that heavenly smile? It was just
like poor Eliza used to smile. Abner, how
dull you've been not to know your own
little Ruth."

"Lord! I believe you're right, Jane.
It's Ruth, sure enough. There's no mistake about that."

They came close to the girls, who tried

to push back, but could not for the pressing crowd. The man came close, and bending his body stuck his face close up into Hester's. She gave a gesture of repulsion and drew herself back.

"How dare you!" she cried. "Let us get out of here."

"How dare I? Listen to her," he cried brokenly, as though his finer feelings had been touched by her words. "How dares a father look on the face of his long-lost child? It grieves me to hear you speak so. I'm your father, child. You are the little Ruth Stout who was lost sixteen years ago. Thank God, I've found you at last."

"Nonsense! I'm Hester Alden. Will you let us pass?" She spoke with dignity and decision, but even as she did so her heart failed her. She was not really Hester Alden. Dim forebodings seized her that she might be this Ruth that some place and at some time had been lost. When this thought came to her, she showed the

"How dare you!" she cried. — *Page 254.*

spirit that Debby Alden would have shown
under similar circumstances. If there were
truth to be known, she wished to know it
all. She would not push the issue aside.
She would know the best or the worst, and
know it at once. She did not flinch now.
The color left her cheek. She drew herself
as far as possible from the revolting features
of the old man. But she waited. Janet
slipped her hand into Hester's and whispered: "Come, let's push back through the
crowd. There's a jam, but we'll be able
to make our way through if we keep at it."

Hester shook her head in negation. She
had no desire to leave now. She wished
to hear what Abner Stout had to say.
Janet could not have dragged her from the
place.

The man had not been in business with
all sorts and conditions of folk for forty years
without reading the girl's expression. He
knew what she feared.   He knew, too,
that it would not be Debby Alden alone

with whom he would have to contend. Hester would be more difficult to manage than the elder woman. He read in her face the dislike for him and the antipathy toward his family. But this did not deter him. He chuckled at her assertion that she was Hester Alden. "So you think, Ruth, my dear child. But, I swear you belong to me. I might have known before. Every time you came into the store I could not take my eyes from you. I couldn't understand. It was nature. Flesh and blood was calling to its own. Jane knew you the minute she clapped her eyes on you. It's strange how things come around. I'd just about given up hope of ever finding you, and here Jane's eyes light on you the first thing. It's great how things do come around."

"Fifteen years. Yes, it was," wailed the old woman. "I know the day. Can I ever forget it? It was the fourth day of June, and poor Eliza was all wrought up and mad

at Abner for something he had said, and
off she starts with Ruth."

Abner affirmed her words with nods and
gestures. He had seized Hester's plump
hand within his bony talons. She made
an effort to withdraw it from his grasp, but
he clung tightly to her.

"Just fifteen years last June," he repeated,
"'Liza went through this place on her way
to Chicago, with little Ruth just a year old."

Jane had come closer and laid her worn,
wrinkled hand upon Hester's arm. The
woman was old and infirm, but age had
not glorified her. She was repulsive. The
girls instinctively shrank from her. She
whimpered and cringed. "'Liza's little girl,"
she began, looking up into Hester's face
with a look meant to be compassionate
and loving, but which was sly and insinuat-
ing.

"My poor, poor sister Eliza," she whined.
"How we did love each other, and how dear
her babies were to me. But little Ruthie

was dearest of all. The dear little child! How I've been worried all these years wondering where you were and if you were provided for. I never could relish my meals, thinking all the time that mebbe my sister and her baby were going hungry. How I've longed to see her and her child no one knows."

She came nearer to the girl, and sticking her face up close said with assumed tenderness: "You're my only sister's little girl. Come, give a loving kiss to your poor Aunt Jane."

Hester gave a gasp of horror and pushed the woman away. "How dare you! Will you move away and allow us to pass?"

Her voice was strong and fearless enough, but her courage went no further than this. Her knees were shaking, and her muscles refused to obey her will. She stood still, unable to move. She might have fallen had not Janet's grasp been upon her and Janet's arm about her waist.

At this the curious crowd back of them parted, and Doctor Heins pushed his way through. Taking hold of Janet and Hester, he turned them about and helped them to make their way through the crowd. But as he left he turned to Abner Stout and said with energy: —

"Let this happen again, Ab, and I'll see to it that you get your just reward! It's outrageous! This heaping insults upon two people who cannot protect themselves!"

With as little commotion as possible he escorted the girls from the store and on to the street. "Hester and Janet are not going to skate this morning," he said to the others of the party. "I wish to talk with them. They'll walk down the street with me."

Without more ado he escorted the girls down a street leading from the skating place. When they came to a less crowded thoroughfare, where conversation was possible, he turned to Hester. "Now tell me how that fuss began and all that old skinflint said to you."

Hester began her story. She was not excited or nervous now, but a great depression was upon her. She would have laughed at the scene had she not felt that truth lay in the man's speech. If she were his daughter, if she belonged to him, he would claim her. She shuddered at the thought. If Abner Stout were her father, he would compel her to live in his home. Joel would be her brother, and the girls, — the thought was revolting. From the innermost fibre of her composition she loathed all that this family stood for; their chicanery, their greed, their cringing and fawning, their disorder of household, and carelessness of attire. They knew neither truth nor friendship if the betrayal of either might add a penny to their hoard. And she, Hester Alden, belonged to them and would be compelled to live with them and make their interests hers!

She began to tremble. In the middle
of her story she flung her arms about the
old doctor's and cried, "You'll never let
them take me, will you?"

He answered her promptly and with conviction. "Never, Hester. I'll abduct you
first myself rather than let that villain take
you. But there is no danger. He's a
subtle one. I don't quite see his purpose
now, but it will be clear later. Come into
my office. The street is not a good place
for tears. I must hear the remainder of
the story, and you must dry those tears.
You do not wish to frighten Aunt Debby
with such a woe-begone countenance."

He led the girls into his private office.
He spoke lightly to reassure them. Yet
he was not satisfied with what he had heard.
He knew that Abner Stout was keen and
crafty. He knew that the man would not
have caused such a scene unless he felt
secure in proving his statement and main-
taining the position which he had assumed.

But why should he wish to claim a child who had no money nor estate? The reason might be that parental affection had asserted itself, but Doctor Heins did not give the man credit for such feeling. He felt that Abner Stout loved nothing so much as he did the circles of silver and gold which poured into his till, and to his ear no music was so sweet as the jingle of the silver as he tested its genuineness with a toss upon the counter.

Doctor Heins heard the story. He laughed and made light of it to encourage Hester and Janet, and kept the girls with him until they had recovered their usual composure. Then he dismissed them with the advice to Hester: "I believe, Hessie, I wouldn't bother your Aunt Debby with that man's story. He may forget it in a day or two, but if he shouldn't and should bother either of you, come to me. I'll send him to the right-about."

"You'll never let him take me?"

"Never." Doctor Heins laughed with assumed gay spirits, squared his shoulders, and said with an air of bravado: "Like the hero in the dime novel, Hessie, I shall allow him to take you over my dead body. There! run home, girls! I've patients awaiting me."

Doctor Heins had learned one fact from hearing the story. Hester knew then that she was not an Alden, and did not belong to her Aunt Debby.

Janet, whose principle was not to desert a friend when that friend was in need, walked with Hester the entire distance home. When they came to the railroad crossing, Hester paused.

"My mother was killed here," she said quietly. "Do you think, Janet, that she was that man's wife — that Jane's sister?"

"Never!" said Janet with conviction. "Any one to look at you could see that you were not of such a family. It's so ridiculous that I can't keep from laughing."

At this she forced a laugh more noticeable for its volume than any suggestion of light spirits.

"But my hair is dark and wavy — " began Hester, determined to probe the matter to the furthest.

"So is mine — much curlier than yours, and about as black. But that's no reason for saying that I belong to them. I defy any one to tell me that I do."

Her voice was so determined and her manner so aggressive that Hester smiled in spite of her grief. Janet continued her nonsense, turning into ridicule Hester's fears, until they reached the Alden home. Hester was so much herself that Debby did not perceive that anything had gone wrong.

She inquired why they had not gone skating. Janet began her story of the skates which would not hold fast to the soles of her shoes. Debby Alden listened. With all her astuteness she did not perceive that

Janet had not answered the question which she had put directly to them.

Janet spent the entire day with Hester. When she saw the troubled look come to her friend's eyes, she grew merry and gay. There was no rest for Hester that day. Janet kept her playing, or singing, or on a hunt for eggs, or a search for pansies in the flower bed which had been covered with straw and boards. Now Janet knew more of Hester's story than Mary Bowerman did, but a sense of honor was within her. She would not by so much as a look let Hester suspect that she knew aught of her history.

After Doctor Heins had escorted the girls from the store, the crowd went about its own affairs. Jane disappeared into the basement kitchen, and made up her savory messes as serenely as though she had not found the child of her dearly beloved sister. Abner went back to the counter and disposed of bargains all day long and far into the night. So far as they were concerned, all interest in Eliza and her child had gone from their minds.

But those who had made up the crowd had seen and heard. The incident had been too unusual not to cause comment. It was discussed in many homes that evening. Hester Alden's history was well known. There was much discussion as to whether she was Abner Stout's daughter. But all advanced this question to substantiate his claims; if she were not his, why should the money-loving, greedy old man wish to claim a penniless girl? It would mean but expense and responsibility to him. This view of the question caused many to believe that he was honest in his words, and that the scene of the morning was unplanned and natural. But the conversation between Abner and his son Joel, which took place that same night after the store had closed, and Jane and the girls were deep in slumber, was a key to the problem.

A smirk of satisfaction was upon the face of the elder man. He rubbed his hands together and chuckled gleefully. The results of the morning's work pleased him. The ability which Joel had shown in this affair was highly gratifying to him. Joel was shrewd; Joel was to be depended upon; Joel knew when to speak and when to be silent. The father thought of these matters and looked with favor upon the oldest child.

"Come," he said ingratiatingly. "Come, sit awhile and talk. I mean to take you into the business, Joel. You've been a good son. I'll change the sign. I will have it read in big gold letters, "Abner Stout and Company."

But Joel would have none of that. "No company for me, father. So help me, no. It's Stout and Stout — full and equal. Herman Loeb has promised me —"

Abner waved his words aside.

"Stout and Stout it shall be, Joel. No

matter. All I have will be yours some day. But about —?" He looked wise and rubbed his hands. "You're sure, my son?"

"Sure, father. I went to the house myself." Abner had heard the story before, but the sounds of the words were as music to his ears. Joel described again the magnificent house with its acres of lawn, and the fine carriages with men in livery.

"And what did you say, Joel?" asked Abner.

"I told them I lived on the East Side. I gave Herman's address. I told them about finding the old newspaper." He made a queer little gesture with his hand. "They thought it was but lately I found it."

"Fifteen years ago — fifteen years ago. Eliza, sorting rags and paper, ran across it. I put it aside — no one can tell, Joel, when such things come in good. Keep a thing seven years, you know."

"I told the woman I thought I knew of

the child — a relative of mine had adopted her and had brought her up like a lady. I'd search for him — I had lost track of him — and I'd come to her with the child."

"And she — she?" Abner leaned eagerly forward.

"She said if I came with the child and with the proofs, she would give me ten thousand dollars cash."

Abner smacked his lips. A smirk of satisfaction spread over his face.

He took from his wallet a dirty, greasy cutting from a newspaper. His eyes glinted with joy as he read. It was an advertisement, fifteen years old, offering a large reward for information concerning a woman named Rosa Williams. Then followed a description of the woman's appearance, dress, and the time and place where she was last known to be.

CHAPTER XIII

HESTER had regained thorough control of herself by the time she went to school Monday morning. She realized that a number of people had witnessed the scene in the store Saturday morning, and that the whole town had heard it by this time. She felt that Miss Watson treated her with a greater kindness than ever before — the woman's way of expressing a silent sympathy. Since the encounter between them in the early fall, Hester had kept as far as possible from Professor Sanderson. Fortunately she was in none of his classes, and never came directly under his authority, so outward harmony at least had been maintained.

But this Monday morning, as he came into the assembly-room to take part in the devotional exercises, she felt that he was

making a study of her. His eyes were upon
her with a critical, uncertain expression.
"He's trying to see if I resemble the Stout
family," she said to herself, and her face
flushed crimson.

Janet Collum and Jane Orr, during
Hester's troubles, maintained the letter
and the spirit of true friendship. They
walked home with Hester, they gave her
choice in the selection of the library books,
and by every power in their means, except
the power of words, they made her feel
that she would always be one of them and
that their love and friendship were about
her now, stronger and more disinterested
than ever.

Orpha was too dull of perception, too
lacking in those finer feelings to realize what
these days meant to Hester. She would
have been willing to do what she could, had
she been able to realize one part of what a
sensitive, proud nature might feel in knowing that she was the subject of discussion

throughout the town, but Orpha knew nothing of such feeling.

Tuesday afternoon Miss Watson sent Hester on an errand to the library. There was a reference to be looked up, and Hester Alden was a reliable person to send forth in search of technical information. She had taken her tablet with her and was about finishing a copy of the distinction between synonyms when Professor Sanderson came into the room. He nodded curtly to the girl, went over to the bookcases, and began his search. He looked up suddenly to address her. "Let me offer my congratulations, Miss Alden."

"Congratulations!" she repeated, looking up in surprise. "I do not quite understand."

He laughed. "I think you would if you'd consider. Of course, we've all heard the news. You are a fortunate young lady, and will be quite an heiress when Abner Stout is called to his fathers. They say that he's worth a million now, and is still collecting."

"His money is nothing to me. I care not how many millions he has." She closed the book and walked to the door. She had no wish to talk with Professor Sanderson on any subject, and this one least of all.

"It will be. If you're his daughter, as he says you are, you'll have your share. I've never known any one yet who refused a hundred thousand dollars. You are very fortunate."

Hester left the room without replying.

"I'd rather have Aunt Debby, and belong to her and her people, than to have ten millions of dollars," she said to herself. "There wouldn't be money enough in the world to make up for leaving her. And I will not. I do not know what I'll do, but I'll not leave her unless they chain me and drag me away."

That thought comforted her. She straightened out her shoulders and raised her head

as she entered the class room. She had no
intention of letting all the school world
know that she was worried and sorrowful.
She would keep her affairs to herself, and
smile and appear as happy as she could.
She had her Aunt Debby's pride in her.

It was toward the last of the week when
her hope and her courage had revived that
she found a letter for her Aunt Debby among
the mail. This was nothing unusual in
itself, but it set her heart to beating rapidly,
for the envelope bore the business card of
Abner Stout. It had been her habit to
stop for the mail on the way from school,
as she did this day.

The evening meal was ready to be served
when she entered the house, and her Aunt
Debby was awaiting her.

"There's letters, auntie," she said, placing
them in Debby Alden's hand.

Debby glanced at them, smiling. "Nothing important," she said. "I'll not bother
reading them now. Come, Hester, while

your meat is hot. I have a veal loaf. I remembered that you like that new recipe I tried."

"I think I like everything you try, Aunt Debby," she said simply as she sat down to the table. Debby Alden smiled. These expressions of affection from Hester pleased her.

"Do you, Hester?" she said. "I'm very glad you do. It wouldn't be a pleasant life for either of us if we did not like what each other did."

She served the meal, ate a little, and then took up the letters which had been lying beside her plate. She read the business heading and smiled grimly. "What is Abner Stout writing to me for? I owe him no bills."

Hester's eyes sought her plate. She made a brave attempt to continue her eating, that her aunt might not observe her perturbation. Debby opened the note, read it, and laughed. Laying the letter aside, she said lightly, "Mr. Stout wishes to see me on business of great importance, and asks me to call at his store to-morrow afternoon."

"Will you go, Aunt Debby?" Hester's eyes were big with alarm. He meant to tell her Aunt Debby. They meant to take her if they could. "But I will not go. They cannot make me," was her thought.

Debby Alden had no suspicion of what that business could be. She looked at Hester and smiled grimly. "Hessie, your Aunt Debby has not spent years studying her Cæsar without learning something. Do you remember the reply that Ariovistus, the German king, gave to Cæsar when the latter bade him come to the Roman camp?"

Hester shook her head. She could not at that moment have said her letters, had she been asked.

"Forgotten already, Hessie? His reply was, 'If Ariovistus wishes anything of Cæsar, he will go to Cæsar; should Cæsar desire anything of Ariovistus, let him go to Ariovistus.' So, if Abner Stout wishes to talk with Debby Alden on business, he must come to Debby Alden."

She looked at Hester and smiled. Then, noticing the child's worn, harassed look, she said: —

"You haven't eaten enough, Hester. Are you ill? Try to eat your veal loaf. Put this hot gravy on it. I'm afraid that high school work is too much for you, Hester. I've thought so all along. I have never looked with favor upon third and fourth floor schoolrooms. Three and four long flights of stairs will not add to the health of young girls. I've told you about going slowly. Are you sure you do not run up and down? Do you take the trouble to put your feet on the steps, as I told you?"

"'Most always, Aunt Debby. Sometimes I forget and go in a hurry."

"Well, I've made up my mind that this

shall be your last year at the high school. You've never been away. It will do you worlds of good. I intend sending you to a boarding-school next winter."

But this, instead of pleasing Hester, as Debby Alden supposed it would, caused her great alarm.

"Aunt Debby, don't ever send me from you. I'd rather be with you than know all the books that were ever printed. You will not send me away?"

"I thought you would enjoy it, Hester. I've been planning all winter. Girls have lovely times at boarding-schools. I thought you would like it."

"I should like the boarding-school well enough and the study, too; but it would mean leaving you, and I don't like that."

"Well, since you feel so about it, I shall not insist, but, —" after a moment's thought, —"we both need a change. I've kept house for almost thirty years. It may do me good to go away for a while. We'll think the matter over, Hester, during the summer. There will be time enough."

The following morning, as Hester was preparing to go to school, Debby Alden came into the hallway and called up to her: "Hester, if you have time, stop into the store and tell Mr. Stout that if he wishes to see me, he will find me at my home any afternoon of the week. Do you hear, Hester?"

"Yes."   There was a pause.   Debby stood waiting to hear Hester's promise. "Wait until I come down, Aunt Debby," she said; "I'll tell you something."

"Very well. You must hurry. It is past eight o'clock now."

She was in the kitchen busy with the breakfast work when Hester came in. "Aunt Debby, if you would just as soon write a note to that man, I'll mail it. I don't like to go in the store, Aunt Debby. I — I — those people make me shudder."

"Just as you will, Hester. Perhaps a

written reply would be more courteous."
She dried her hands and went to the writ-
ing-desk in the living-room, where she
wrote a note to Abner Stout, in which she
replied to his request as the old German
had replied centuries before to the Roman
leader.

Miss Watson had spent years in the
schoolroom with young people. She understood them as thoroughly as she did the
text-books from which she had been teaching for twenty years. She had heard of the
scene of the previous Saturday morning.
She appreciated the position in which Hester was placed, and knew what a proud
and sensitive nature would suffer under
conditions such as these. She saw the
effort which Hester made to keep a smiling,
cheerful countenance to the school, and
admired her for it, as one must ever admire strength of character and self-control.

Miss Watson was a great student, and
loved study in any form. Yet she was

liberal-minded enough to put a proper
estimate upon books. She knew that
they could never be first in affairs of life.
Lessons were very well, but there were
times when they should go to the wall.
She believed that this time had come for
Hester. The child was not in a condition
to study. Yet Miss Watson could not tell
her so and excuse her from recitations.
That would throw Hester's thoughts back
upon herself and set the hundred pupils
surmising and wondering. School had
barely been called when Miss Watson spoke
to Hester. "Miss Alden, would you and
Miss Orr go on an errand for me? I've
left my books at home." She named the
books, and told the girls where in her house
they could be found. Hester and Jane set
forth. Miss Watson lived on the South
Side. A walk to her home took them
across the river bridge and down long,
broad streets for a great distance. They
went on their way rejoicing, for the morn-

ing was fine and the lessons left in the schoolroom were tedious and long.

Jane was in the best of humor, and was a constant source of droll, good-natured talk. When they turned down Eighth Street, which led to the bridge, they met Ralph coming from the college building and hurrying to the athletic grounds.

Jane stopped to look at his retreating form. Her face was expressive of the greatest admiration. "Ralphie is the best boy," she said. "I'm always glad I have him. Girls without brothers do not know what they miss."

"Oh, yes, they do! I've always wanted a brother, ever since I was a little girl, and since I've grown up, I want one more than ever. I'd give —" She stopped suddenly. Perhaps she had a brother, after all. But not such a brother as Ralph. Before her came a picture of Joel Stout with a smirk upon his face, and his fawning, ingratiating manner. The thought of his presence, redolent with musk, and his talon-like fingers, which showed no knowledge of manicure or brush, was repulsive.

Quick as a flash, Jane observed Hester's change of expression and understood its cause. "But every one cannot have a brother like Ralph," she said quickly. "There wouldn't be enough to go around. I'm one of the lucky girls, and I don't intend being selfish. I'll divide whenever you need a brother, Hester; just send me word, and I'll lend you Ralph."

Hester laughed. "What would Ralph say about that? He might object."

"No, indeed. That is what makes him what he is. He does what I ask without even asking why."

"He must be uncommon," said Hester, with conviction.

"He is," responded Jane, earnestly. Then Jane laughed at herself for being such a braggart about her brother. From this she went on to other conversation, turning each detail about that Hester might see the brighter side, or repeating incidents that were far removed from matters which troubled Hester. Jane understood Miss Watson's purpose in sending them on this errand. She did not hurry, but loitered by the roadside to see if by chance there might be some early green on the protected side of the hill. The view from the bridge attracted, and she hung over the railing for several minutes to enjoy its beauty. So, by her skilful loitering, it was almost dismissal time before they reëntered the class room.

"Miss Watson will reprimand us," said Hester. "We have been gone twice as long as was necessary."

"Don't you believe it," said Jane, with conviction. "Hasn't she always advocated our cultivating a love for outside life? If she speaks to me about the time we spent in our errand, I'll explain to her that I was drinking in the beauties of nature. She'll not resist that." Jane smiled blandly at this, walked up to Miss Watson's desk, deposited the book, and said: "It was so beautiful on the bridge, Miss Watson, that I could not hurry. I walked up the old road a little way. It was so inviting. I was the laggard — not Hester. She did her best to hurry me."

"You did very well, Jane. I'm glad that you saw fit to loiter." Hester heard the words with surprise. Miss Watson was charming, and the pupils loved her, but her most devoted admirers had never been able to say that her discipline was not rigid. What had come to her that she was taking matters so lightly?

While she was wondering at the change in Miss Watson, the letter she had mailed that morning had been delivered to Abner Stout, and he and his son had eagerly devoured it.

They read and looked at each other. Joel spoke first. "What do you think about that, father?"

"Joel, I'm not sure what to think. This Miss Alden, Joel, is not like other women. She will be — be — difficult to manage, Joel, I'm thinking. Why, she has kept this secret for fifteen years." He looked up at his son as though he expected some show of surprise upon hearing this statement. Abner Stout stood in awe of Miss Alden. This feeling was brought about by the fact that she had trusted no one, and had kept her own secrets. Surely that showed strength and power not found in the average person.

"Do you think she knows all this, father?" Abner shook his head in negation.

"No, Joel. She does not know all. I'm pretty sure of that. If she did, our plans would be worth —" He snapped his fingers. "But she knows something. She so much as told that Bowerman woman who lives down her way. She knows that the girl's people are able to pay for all this care and clothes and sending to school.

No woman would take all this trouble for nothing, Joel."

Joel was not easily convinced. He could not understand why Debby Alden would not make herself known to the child's family. Fifteen years is a long time to wait. He expressed himself to his father.

Abner saw the matter in a different light. It was his opinion that Debby Alden knew only that the child belonged to wealthy people, and had perhaps a general idea as to their whereabouts. He believed, also, that the woman expected Hester to fall heir to immense wealth. With the child under her control, she could manipulate matters as she wished. That she was awaiting a proper time for the climax of affairs, he did not doubt. His mind and training had been such that he could not conceive of a person who could sacrifice for the sake of affection, or from a high idea of duty to one's fellow-creatures. Because he could not conceive of a nature such as

Debby Alden's, he misconstrued her acts in his mind, and placéd her upon the same level as himself and his son.

They discussed fully the reason for Debby Alden replying to them as she had done. The note was courteous, so far as that went, but it was also independent. That she was not ready to cringe and make terms with them was what they read between the lines. She had faith in herself and her ability to maintain the position she had assumed, the note told them. They admired her subtlety and her bravado, for they did not for an instant think that Hester had not repeated to her Aunt Debby all that had taken place that Saturday morning in the store. Again, they were unable to conceive of a girl who would keep such matters to herself, and suffer silently, rather than cause a moment of uneasiness to one whom she loved.

Joel was eager to sit down at once and answer Miss Alden's note, but his father would not hear to it. He shook his head solemnly, while his keen eyes glinted. "It would not do, Joel. It would not do. We will call upon Miss Debby Alden, since it is the only way, but I talk better when I have my own people about me. I'd rather she came here; I'm on my own ground when I'm in my own store and my own house. Yet, since there's no way of getting around it, we'll go, but not to-day. She'll think that we're over anxious, and I don't want her to think that. We'll go to-morrow, Joel. We'll not walk. We'll drive. There's times when spending a dollar is money in your pocket. And to-morrow will be one of the times."

"I'll write and tell her we'll be there to-morrow," said Joel, seizing his pen. Joel, who could write with many flourishes and much shading on the downward strokes, looked upon his penmanship as his one accomplishment, and was always eager to flaunt it in the face of an admiring public.

But Abner laid a restraining hand upon the young man's arm. "What's the use of writing?" he asked. "You act as though you had lost your mind. The very last thing we want that Alden woman to know is that we're coming to talk business with her. Take her unawares and off her guard, and there's no telling how much she'll let slip. But let her know that we're coming, and she'll have her mind made up as to what's best to tell and what's best to keep to one's self. She'd have a few sharp words ready on the end of her tongue. She's a mighty smart woman, and as deep as the Lord ever made any one. But you'd let her know, and give her a chance to be ready for us." He glowered at his son, and let his voice ring out sharply. "That's what you would do with your infernal letter-writing. But, you're never happy unless you've got a pen in your hand. There's one thing you've got to keep in your mind when you deal with this Alden woman; that's to think twice and speak once. And there's another business rule you'd do well to get into your head: save the ink in your own well, and let the other fellow do the writing."

With such practical advice Abner Stout closed his heart-to-heart talk with his son.

CHAPTER XIV

THE story of Abner Stout's claim upon Hester Alden came to Miss Richards. She was greatly troubled for Debby's sake. She would not have given the story credence had she not remembered Debby's words but a short time before in regard to Hester's parentage. She deliberated some time before she drove down to the Alden home, uncertain whether Debby might wish her to come at such a time.

But after thinking over the matter, she decided to do by this friend as she would wish to be done by, were their positions interchanged. She had not expected to find Debby either in tears or sitting down bewailing, for such had never been the way of the Aldens, and this last member of the family was capable of great self-control, but she was surprised to find her exceedingly cheerful and with a buoyancy of spirit in her manner and voice which came to Debby only when she was feeling her best.

"I'm glad you came," was her greeting, as she came to the gate to welcome her guest. "I have just finished my weekly cleaning. When I saw the carriage come over the hill, I wished it was some one to spend the day with me." She turned to the coachman. "Come after Miss Richards sometime this evening, Herrick. She will spend the day with me." She laughed, and waved aside all Miss Richards's words about coming only for a call.

"This day suits me best of all," she said. "I've put my house in order and have a nice fat hen ready for the roaster. Hester and I cannot manage such a large fowl. It will be an act of charity to stay and help us dispose of it."

They went together into the great old-fashioned living-room. The windows commanded a view of the road from town as it descended

the hill after crossing the tracks. There
was a bright-striped rag carpet upon the
floor, white dimity curtains at the windows,
and scarlet bunches of geraniums.

"Have you any sewing on hand?" asked
Miss Richards, as she sat in the great wooden
rocker by the west window.

"I've cut out some shirt-waists for Hester, enough to last her through the summer.
I'm not in a hurry to finish them. She will
not begin to wear them until summer is
really here. So I mean to take my time.
I'm putting my best needlework on them.
I think it looks daintier than so much
bought lace."

Miss Richards nodded her agreement.

"There's nothing daintier than handwork. Get out the waists, Debby, and I'll
take a few stitches. I always like to feel
that I have a little interest in Hester."

"You always will have, Eva. Hester
feels the same toward you. I believe, after
me, that she loves you. I told her about

going to school next winter. She likes the
idea of school well enough, but declares she
will not leave me."

Her face lighted up. Hester's words had
pleased her more than any other thing the
girl could have done. She left the room
to get the sewing, leaving her guest alone
for a few minutes.

Miss Richards was in a dilemma. Debby
did not know then of what had occurred in
Stout's store the previous Saturday morning! The story was the property of the
entire town, and had been rolled between
hundreds of tongues and turned about like
a delectable morsel, while she who was the
most vitally interested knew nothing of
the matter. Miss Richards understood the
reason for this. No one would have come
to Debby with this story, for she was one
of whom many stood in awe, while Hester
had kept the matter to herself, lest her aunt
should be unnecessarily worried.

"There may nothing come of it," thought

Miss Richards. "The Stouts may have acted so for some purpose of their own, and with no idea of carrying the matter further."

Debby came in at this with her arms filled with shirt-waists.

"If you will make French knots, Eva," she said, "I shall be glad. Mine never look quite as well as yours."

Miss Richards consented, and soon the two women were interested in the sewing, with now and then a sentence by way of conversation.

"I had a letter this week which was rather out of the ordinary," said Debby, pausing, as she snapped a new thread from the spool.

Miss Richards looked up from her work, her face expressing her interest.

"From Abner Stout. He wished to see me on a matter of business, and asked me to call at his store."

"Did you, Debby?" There was a trace of anxiety in Eva Richards's voice.

"Scarcely. I have no business interests
with him. If he wishes to see me, he knows
where I live. I sent him word to that
effect."

"When was that?"

"I mailed the letter Tuesday morning."

"And this is Friday. Has he called here
yet?"

"No, I fancy he will not. No doubt he
had some goods in the store he thought he
might be able to persuade me into taking.
I'm confident that his business was of no
more importance than that. Don't you
fancy so?"

Miss Richards made no reply. But her
lack of response awakened no suspicion in
Debby's mind.

The conversation languished, for Miss
Richards's mind was busy with her question of ethics, as to whether she should or
should not make known to her friend the
business which Abner Stout might have in
common with her. To touch upon an-

other's personal affairs is a delicate matter, and Eva Richards questioned what was best to do, and hesitated between two decisions.

But the decision was taken from her. Debby looked up from her work, and across the field to the road over the hill, along the mountain side. "Another carriage coming over Paddy's Run road," she said. "I wonder if it is coming here. If it is, I'll have this as a reception day." She laughed lightly as she added: "Perhaps it is Abner Stout coming to pay me a visit. If it is, I'm sure I shall be overwhelmed with the honor. You must assist me to receive him with due ceremony, Eva."

Miss Richards laid down her sewing. Her hands trembled with nervousness. "It may be, Debby. It may be, and if it is, I must tell you what his business is. It is not right that you should meet him unprepared. He's too subtle, too crafty, for you to deal with. I must tell you why he comes."

"Yes," said Debby Alden. She threaded her needle and took a buttonhole stitch as firmly and as evenly as though her guest had made no comment more pretentious than one on the conditions of the weather. "Yes," she repeated, for Miss Richards had hesitated.

"I thought you knew. I gave no thought but Hester would come directly home to tell you. Poor child, I suspect she wished to spare you, and — perhaps she did not believe it after all."

Then without interruption she told Debby Alden of the scene between Hester and Abner Stout, and how Doctor Heins had led the girls away and had spoken sharply to the man.

Debby Alden listened without comment. She had continued her buttonhole-making while the story was told. The sole expression of the anger and indignation which were filling her heart was shown in the quick, sharp way in which she drew her thread. Miss Richards understood her well, and expected nothing more than this.

"I felt that you must be prepared when you met this man, or I would not have told you," said Miss Richards, as she concluded the story.

"I understand. I understand."

Laying aside her work, Debby moved nearer to the window, that she might watch the progress of the carriage as it by turns appeared and disappeared as the road rose on the brow of the hill or lay hidden in the depressions of the valley.

"They have turned down between here and Bowermans'," she said at last. "One of us is to be favored." She did not leave her place at the window until she saw that the carriage had stopped at her own gate.

"You are right, Eva. Abner Stout and his son, Joel, in all the glory of bright ties and plaid suits are about to honor us with a call. They have hired a livery rig. My! what extravagance!"

Miss Alden opened the door in response to their knock, and the two men entered without invitation, selected the easiest chairs in the room, and seated themselves, while Debby Alden stood looking upon them with an inscrutable smile upon her lips and a dignity of manner which would have put to rout the self-assertive manners of less confident persons.

They had arrayed themselves regardless of expense. They had done so with the intent of impressing Miss Alden. They impressed, but not just in the way they thought. She observed each detail of their attire, for it clamored aloud to be noticed; the room became filled with the odor of a powerful scent. As their hands jangled their many-sealed watch chains, it was evident that their nails were in mourning for the death of an orange-wood stick, a file, and a brush.

"I got your letter Tuesday," began Abner. His present position was so unusual that it confused him. A perspiration broke upon him. He mopped his brow, and the odor of musk was wafted with the wave of his handkerchief. If only Miss Alden, grave and serene and quiet, would not stand and look at him! He repeated his statement with a slight variation in order of the words.

"Your letter reached me Tuesday."

"So I suppose. The United States mail is generally reliable."

"You said that we would find you home when we came."

"So I remember having written. My being present now proves the truth of my statement."

This was too much for Abner. He could not grasp the gentle irony of such speech. He had dealt with many people, but never one who spoke so enigmatically, and smiled so inscrutably as Miss Debby Alden. He knew no precedent in the dealing with such people. For the time he was disconcerted, and blurted out, "I suppose Ruthie — that is, Hester, — told you that we talked with her?"

"Miss Hester and I have never discussed you in any way. There has never been occasion to do so."

"Didn't she say what business was bringing us here?"

"As I have said, my niece and I have never discussed you. Therefore it would be impossible for her to tell me the reason for this call, even should it chance that she knew it."

Abner smiled sardonically. Not for one instant did he believe that Hester Alden had not related in detail all that had transpired that Saturday morning. He pressed his thin lips, and looked at Miss Alden with a sneer.

"She knows it all right from A to Z, and you do, too. I see no use in trying to pretend you don't. The truth's bound to come out sooner or later. I'll see that it does. You've kept my little girl for fifteen years, and now I mean to have her." Then feeling that a show of emotion would be in keeping with his part, he let his head fall on his breast, assumed what he thought was a sorrowful expression; which was not dissimilar to that which a starving wolf might assume when it was desirous of winning the confidence of a young lamb. "No one knows how dreadful these fifteen years have been to me," he said brokenly. "No one knows how I feel about this."

The serenity of Miss Alden was not disturbed. Feeling that some reply was expected of her, she said calmly, "If you felt as bad as you look, it must have been dreadful."

She had no sooner spoken than the double meaning in her words came to her. She had not intended saying all that the speech implied. She could not restrain a smile. She glanced quickly at Miss Richards and saw that her eyes were twinkling.

Although Abner Stout had spent his life in America, and Joel had been educated in its great public school system, neither were able to grasp the subtleties of its humor. Miss Alden's words were accepted in good part.

"Yes; that's just how I felt. I have spent fifteen years grieving over the loss of that child, and here she's been comfortable all this time. You did wrong, Miss Alden, in not publishing in the papers about the child and her mother. I don't doubt that the law would hold you guilty of fraud. However, that is past and gone. You may have acted in ignorance. But whatever led you to it, I'm willing to overlook it all. All that I can think of now is that the girl known as Hester Alden is my little daughter, Ruth. I know that you'll be glad to hear that the fatherless has found a father."

"Well, no, Mr. Stout. I cannot honestly say that such a piece of news would awaken any such feeling."

"No?" He looked upon her in surprise as though to say: "Is it possible? Do you lack all natural feeling? Are you less than human?"

She returned his furtive glance with a steady gaze. He let his head sink upon his breast as if overcome by her lack of proper feeling.

"Haven't I made it plain to you?" he continued after a moment's pause. "This girl you call Hester Alden is my child Ruth. She is the child of my wife Eliza who was killed at the crossing. Ruth must come to her father's house. There'll be room for her. There is no one, Miss Alden, so near as your own flesh and blood."

"I agree heartily with you, Mr. Stout. No one can be so dear to us as our own people."

Abner, believing that such a concession was a show of weakness, became encouraged and continued his talk, interspersing it with many gestures and sidewise airing of his hands. In the earnestness of his conversation he drew nearer and nearer to Debby Alden, until he stood directly before her, his sharp eyes peering up into her face, and his talon-like fingers almost touching her. Debby Alden drew herself erect and moved back. The man was too self-satisfied to read the repulsion which her movement manifested. But Joel understood. He laid a detaining hand upon his father's arm, and, drawing him back, took up the thread of conversation himself. "My father is so excited that he forgets himself. What he means to say, Miss Alden, is that he's ready to take Ruth — that is, Hester, and take care of her as he does his other children. It will be a great saving to you, as it costs something to keep a girl her age. Father knows that, but he'll do what's right for Ruthie."

"He is surely very kind — very generous," Debby Alden replied.

"Of course, we know you'll miss her and

hate to part with her, but then, there's the money it has cost to keep her. There's no use of your having the trouble longer. This is Friday. If Hester could come to her new home Saturday evening —"

"Sabbath, her first day at home! How lovely! How appropriate!" cried Abner, rubbing his hands together.

"I will drive down for her myself. I will not ask her to walk."

"I would not take that trouble. Consider the livery bill," said Miss Alden, dryly.

But Joel explained that on such an occasion as this, money would not be considered. Hester would receive a royal welcome and be given her proper place in the household of Abner Stout.

Miss Alden allowed them to finish their story before she addressed them. "You have talked a great deal of nonsense. Hester Alden is Hester Alden, and will remain so. I cannot understand your reason for coming to me with such a story, but I take

it for granted that you have some purpose
in view. The subject is stopped right here,
also your discussion of it among the people
who come to your store. If you so much
as address the child again, I shall take
means to prevent her being annoyed. If
that is all the business you have with me,
I'll bid you good afternoon."

She moved to the outside door and laid
her hand on the knob, as about to open it
for the egress of the callers. But the two
were not to be put aside so. Abner straightened his shoulders and said sharply: "We
will not go. We will not be put off in this
way. There's a law, madam. Remember
that there is a law which will put aside
your weak words."

Again Joel calmed him, and, turning to
Miss Alden, said, "You think we are talking,
but we mean to have our little Ruthie. If
you give her up without trouble, very well,
but if you don't, then we'll have the law
make you give her up. We've friends in

New York who knew my mother and all
about the time she disappeared. We can
prove that she was the woman who was
killed and brought here. We'll prove it."

"Do you think so?" Miss Alden showed
admirable self-control. She was not so
much alarmed as she was angry.

She continued, as she opened wide the
door: "Prove it if you can. I am quite
sure that you cannot do so. For," with a
sweet smile and gracious bow, "I know
more about Hester's people than you suspect. Not a drop of your blood is in her
veins."

"I shall have the law on you. I shall
employ a lawyer."

"As you will, but it seems a pity to
waste a fee. Good afternoon."

They would have said more, but Debby
did not wait to hear. She closed the door
after her, and turned to Miss Richards.

"Are you surprised at my discourtesy?"
she asked with a smile. "Those people

"I KNOW MORE ABOUT HESTER'S PEOPLE THAN YOU SUSPECT."
Page 310.

have always been offensive to me, but when
they enter my house ready with lies for
my undoing, they merit more than discourtesy."

"But, Debby, are you sure? It couldn't
be possible that these people are correct?"

"Utterly impossible. Does Hester look
or act as they do? Does she show one of
their traits?"

"No, but —"

"There is no question about it. I am
sure of my statement. Hester hasn't one
drop of Stout blood in her veins. But
we've spent the greater part of the afternoon in the discussion. I must see to my
dinner, if you will excuse me."

The freshman class was dismissed early
Friday afternoon. Hester Alden was trudg-
ing along over the hill when she saw a
carriage come down the lane between her
home and the Bowermans'. She felt at once
that it must be Abner Stout, and her heart
failed her. In a few minutes the carriage

passed her. Joel was driving, while Abner was talking excitedly and gesticulating with both hands, the palms upturned. She glanced at him and hurried on. As she entered the kitchen, Debby Alden was just taking the chicken from the oven. She looked up and smiled.

"You're in time, Hester. You did not have much of a lunch to-day, so I thought I'd have an early dinner. Miss Richards is in the living-room, Hester. Go in and speak to her."

Hester had stood like one dumfounded. She could not account for her Aunt Debby's lightness of manner and cheerfulness of voice. Without a word she passed into the living-room.

Miss Richards observed the troubled look in the girl's eye, and understood the reason. She arose to greet her.

"Your friends have been here, Hester, and your Aunt Debby has sent them right about. Don't give them another serious thought. But this evening, after I'm gone, tell your Aunt Debby what happened last week. It is right that she should know." She drew Hester to her and kissed her. At the words the troubled look left the girl's eyes, and she gave a sigh of relief.

CHAPTER XV

DEBBY ALDEN did a great deal of thinking during the days which followed, but she did not put her thoughts into action, as she wished to be on the defensive rather than the offensive side should the subject of Hester's parentage again be brought up. She knew not what course Abner Stout might take. She did not believe one word of their story, yet she could not understand why they should wish to take Hester into their family. She had a feeling that something lay back of their action, and determined that she would keep herself in touch with all they did, in the hope of discovering the reason for this scheme.

She was not long left in doubt as to the stand they would take. Within a week she

received a formal notice from Hinter and
Hendig, attorneys-at-law, asking her to appear before them and give reason for the
detention in her home of one Ruth Stout,
generally known as Hester Alden. The
date for her appearance was fixed for the
following Saturday morning at eleven-thirty.

Debby read the letter at the supper table,
for Hester, as usual, had brought the mail
home with her. She smiled grimly, and
after a moment's hesitation tossed the single
sheet of paper across to Hester.

"There's interesting reading for you,"
she said. Hester read and then looked up
in alarm. "You will not let them take
me, Aunt Debby? I will not go with
them."

"Don't give that a thought. There is
not a possibility of your going. I'm sorry
for them that they employed Hinter and
Hendig. They will have a pretty fee to
pay. Giving up money is worse on Abner
Stout than drawing blood."

"They must think they can make me go, Aunt Debby, or they would not employ such men. Perhaps they know more than they told you. They may know —"

"One thing they do not know, Hessie. That one thing, no one but myself knows. I have no fear of what either Abner Stout or his son Joel can do."

She dropped the subject then and asked Hester concerning the lessons of the day. They had been uncertain regarding a sentence in Latin, and Debby wished to know how the Latin teacher had translated it.

The subject of what Abner Stout might do was not brought up again until Friday morning. Despite her aunt's encouragement, Hester was worried. She could not understand why these men should care to claim her unless she really belonged to them. This lack of understanding made her fearful. Then, too, she was inclined to believe that her Aunt Debby's confidence was partly assumed for her encouragement. She tried to keep her mind upon her lessons, but her efforts resulted in failure. Her recitations were scarcely worthy of the name. Miss Watson understood, and made the way easier for her by explaining matters to the other teachers.

Jane Orr and Janet Collum walked with her on her way home, and brought out their gayest spirits, and kept them on dress-parade for Hester's benefit. She could not be dull in their company, and before she knew what was happening the Stouts were forgotten and she was laughing as light-hearted and merry as the others.

When Hester started to school Friday morning, Debby Alden came out to the porch and handed her two notes enclosed in small envelopes. "One to Mrs. Orr and one to Mrs. Collum, Hessie. Give them to the girls to carry to their mothers. I've asked permission for Jane and Janet to spend the day with you. You know I must be in town to-morrow, and it will be dull for you to be alone."

"May I go with you, Aunt Debby? I'll worry dreadfully while you are gone."

"That would be very foolish, to worry about nothing. I cannot see that you will gain by it. No, Hester; you may not go. Now, don't look so at me or I shall say yes when my judgment says the other thing." She put her hands before her eyes as though to shut out the face, then laughed and turned toward the door. But before entering she turned to smile and wave good-by.

Kate Bowerman's ears had been tickled with the news of the disturbance which Abner Stout was about to make. She set forth this Friday morning on what she called a visit of sympathy for Debby Alden. She found her in the kitchen, rolling out a batch of cookies, while a heap of some fresh from the oven were spread out on the bread cloth on the table to cool.

Kate came in without knocking, and

seating herself near the table helped herself to a cookie. "Sour milk?" she asked
by way of greeting.

"Good morning, Kate. Yes, I used sour
milk and soda. I like it better."

"I can always taste soda," was the rejoinder. "I've never seen the cook yet
who could fool me on soda. It always
leaves a sort of slippery taste." She had
finished her cookie by this time, and reached
for another.

Debby did not reply. She had long since
learned the wisdom of keeping quiet when
the issue was of as little importance as this.
Then, too, she knew Kate's weakness in
always taking the opposite side of any
question. She did not doubt that had she
told Kate that baking-powder had been
used, Kate would have begun an argument
in favor of soda.

Mrs. Bowerman talked for some minutes
on the subject, munching cookies all the
while, and then she turned to Debby with

the remark, "I hear you are having trouble with the Stouts."

"You've been misinformed. I'm not having trouble with them." She rolled out another ovenful of cakes and prepared to cut them.

"You haven't!" Kate looked incredulous. "Well, from all the reports that I've heard, you must be having a peck of trouble with them."

"Not a bit. On the contrary, they are having trouble with me."

Kate sniffed, stuck out her tongue — as was her habit when surprised or excited. But she had come over there to sympathize with Debby Alden, and sympathize she would, whether Debby desired it or not.

"Well, either way you put it, it's bad enough. It would have been an excellent thing, Debby Alden, if you had listened to my advice years ago. I was against you keeping the child. You know that. Here, after all your trouble and expense, it turns out that she belongs to that dirty, low set of people. It wouldn't have seemed so bad if you'd discovered her parents and found them to be good reliable folks. But your time and money wasted on —" She did not finish her sentence, but made a gesture of disgust as she reached forth to take another cookie.

Debby made no reply. She rolled her dough with more than her usual amount of energy, and cut the cakes with a manner indicating that she was putting her power of self-control to the test. Kate, heedless of the signs, continued: "If she belonged to one of the good old families, it would have been different. I set store by what stock folks come from. There's nothing like old families, I say. Don't you agree to that, Debby?"

"Oh, yes, if they're not so old that they're mouldy," she replied, with seeming indifference. "When it comes to that, I prefer new ones."

She stooped before the oven, dish towel in hand. Her cheeks were flushed with heat.

"You've a sharp tongue to-day, Debby. Do for pity's sake learn to control it, or you'll be ugly-tempered before you are an old woman. I've always disliked that kind of old folks, and I've watched myself like a hawk. But to go back to our subject about Hester's being a Stout. Do you know, I've noticed the resemblance for years, but I hated to speak —"

"Then do not do it if you have disliked it so. As far as Hester is concerned, she is an Alden — nothing more nor less. Not a word that you can say or leave unsaid can alter that in the least. So why not drop the subject, Kate?"

"My! but you're touchy this morning, Debby. A neighbor cannot come in with a word of sympathy but you flare up like a house afire." She rose, and wrapping her shawl about her, moved toward the door.

"There's no use of trying to talk with you in such a humor; I'll go."

"Come again, Kate, when Hester is not the subject to be discussed." Repenting of her hasty speech, she added, as she piled a dish high with cakes: "Take these home for Sam's dinner. He used to like my sour-cream cookies."

So the treaty of peace was signed between them, and Kate went home by way of the lane, lest her plate of cakes should suffer should she attempt climbing the fences.

Janet and Jane came home from school with Hester. They were rejoicing in the possession of several new recipes, and were eager to try them.

"Mother wouldn't care if I tried them at home," said Janet, "but the cook's so cranky about our going into the kitchen. Edith Rank wrote this recipe for me. She says it's fine. There's not another girl in school who can make fudge like Edith."

"There's no cook here to bother us," said Debby. "You may try the whole batch of recipes."

"I said Aunt Debby wouldn't care," said Jane, addressing Janet.

"Thank goodness, there's no cook to fear!" cried Janet. "Let's begin the instant we have finished supper, and, Aunt Debby, let us have supper early."

There was no refusing Janet. Her plans were carried out. Debby Alden took part in the making of the fudge and caramels as though she, too, were going through a new experience of the freedom of the kitchen. Janet and Jane understood without explanation the reason for their invitation at this particular time. They were so overflowing with energy and high spirits that Hester was well employed keeping up with them.

Debby Alden started forth to town immediately after breakfast the following morning. The three girls went with her to the gate.

"We'll have a lovely dinner ready for you," was Jane's parting words. "I'll get it myself."

Janet groaned. "You had better bring some dyspepsia tablets along, Aunt Debby, if Jane does the cooking. I'll bake a cake, myself. You'll be sure of one good bite."

It was Jane's turn to groan.

"If you intend eating Janet's cake, you had better bring a doctor with you. Dyspepsia tablets would count nothing against her angel-food cake."

"I did not say I would make an angel-food cake."

"No, but your cake would make an angel of any one who would eat it."

With the laughter following such mild bantering of each other, Debby Alden left them and went into town.

Her first visit was to Doctor Heins. He knew what had taken place during the last week, and expected her visit. He ushered her into his private office, saw that she was seated, and after adjusting his glasses peered at her and began the conversation with, "Well, what are we going to do about Hester?"

"They can do nothing, Doctor. But their efforts have set me thinking. While I am living, I can settle such matters. But sometime the question of Hester's people must come up again. It must come up. Some day she must know, and the papers must be so arranged that it will be attended to whether I am here or not."

"Then you are sure she does not belong to the Stouts?"

"Quite sure. I know it, and you do also, Doctor Heins."

He blinked, cleaned his glasses, and looked at her with surprise.

"Indeed, Debby Alden, I know nothing at all about it, and never for one moment did I suspect that you did."

"Yes, you know as much as I." She paused a moment, and then resting her

arms on the office table, she leaned over
and spoke to him in a tone of voice and
expression quite different from the independent, self-reliant, fearless ones which
marked the Aldens.

"You, as a doctor, hear many things in
confidence. Because I believe I can trust
you, I am going to bring to your mind
several incidents of the time you came to
my home, when Hester's mother was
brought there. Do you remember what it
was you said as you held the dead woman's
hands in yours?"

"I do not, Debby. I have so much of
that work."

"I remember." She paused again, and
then bending closer to him, in a voice
almost a whisper, repeated his words of
fifteen years before. He looked perplexed.
"Does it not come to you that there might
be something else to cause the condition
which you remarked?" she said.

His expression changed. "Why, of

course. I gave it no thought. But you are right, Debby. And you knew this from that time?"

"I discovered it from something which occurred while she was sitting at my table. There is no question about it."

"There cannot be. Then the advertisement for the child's people was a misrepresentation. No wonder no one ever came to claim her."

"I did not attend to the advertising. I did not misrepresent the matter. The town officers attended to that."

"Then she is not a Stout. What will you do to convince them? Will you tell them who she is?"

"No. The story would be abroad before the day had passed. Mr. Laffler has always attended to my business affairs. He will attend the meeting with Hintner and Hendig. He attended to the matter when I legally adopted Hester."

"You really adopted her? Well, that

clinches the matter for Abner. He could
not take her from you, even were she the
Ruth he claims her to be. We never knew,
Debby, whether you attended to having
the papers drawn up or not. You never
mentioned the matter to any one."

"I did not know that my affairs would
interest any one," she said. "My purpose
here to-day was not to tell you that. But
knowing what you do of Hester's mother,
you understand that sometime my girl
must know. If she should ever think of
marrying, she would have to be told."

"Yes, yes. It would not do at all. But
how are you going to mend matters?"

"You and I may be gone before that
time. I wish you to write down and sign
what you know of the child's mother. I
will do the same. I will have those papers
put away with the injunction that they
must be read when she reaches the age of
discretion."

The doctor nodded his approval of the

plan. "I'll attend to that at once, Debby. I'll bring the paper to you before Monday."

"Very well. I am to meet Mr. Laffler at his office. I presume he is through with the conference by this time."

On her way to the lawyer's office she met Abner and his son. The elder man was sawing the air sidewise with his upturned palms, his shoulders were hunched, and his sharp face stuck forward. As he passed Miss Alden, he gave her a look in which hatred, fear, and admiration were alike in evidence.

On arriving at the office, Miss Alden found that there had been no difficulty in Mr. Laffler's way. Hintner and Hendig, on being informed that Hester had been legally adopted, dropped the case at once. It may have been that they were glad to do so, for they were not in sympathy with Abner Stout and his method of business, and they believed, with the majority of the townspeople, that Hester was happier and better with Debby Alden than she could be with the other family.

Debby started home immediately. She appreciated Hester's feelings during the morning. The girls had had dinner prepared for some time, and were eagerly watching from the windows for her coming. As Debby turned from the main road, Jane saw her first. With a tact born of unselfishness, she cried: "There she is! Hester, run to meet her while Janet and I serve the dinner."

Hester was already from the kitchen and flying down the garden path. The two met at the gate. Hester flung her arms about Miss Alden. "Tell me, Aunt Debby, — did —"

She could not finish. Her fear of the answer was so great that her lips trembled and her eyes filled with tears. Debby Alden laughed and drew Hester's arm about her, holding her hand in her own. "No, they didn't, and they never will," she replied, nodding her head gayly. "Didn't I tell you, silly child, that there was nothing to fear? The court gave you to me with the name of Alden. The Stouts, from a mere whim of their own, cannot take you from me. So," with a pressure of the hand, "you are compelled to stay with me, whether you wish to or not."

"Oh!" Then, as might be expected of a girl who would not cry when there was reason enough for tears, Hester sobbed aloud, but her face was smile-wreathed all the while. Debby let her have her cry out. They had come to the steps of the side porch, and stood there for a moment, Hester leaning her head against Debby Alden's shoulder and with Debby Alden's arms about her. When she was able to control herself, she looked up and asked: "Aunt Debby, will you tell me something? Do I belong to those people? Am I Joel's sister?"

"No; you are not, and they know it. I

cannot understand why they wished to take you from me. No doubt they had a selfish reason back of their efforts." She waited a moment. The time was one suitable for confidence.

"There is one matter I must speak to you about, Hester, and then we'll never mention the subject again. I and Doctor Heins know something about your mother's people that no one else knows or needs to know. I may not always be with you, so I have made provisions for that. I will give Mr. Laffler a written account which Doctor Heins and I have signed. But I do not wish you to read that, Hester, unless it is absolutely necessary. I'd much prefer that you would remain in ignorance of your people. Yet, sometime, the occasion may arise when it will be best for you to know. I wish you would never marry, Hester; but if the time comes when you give serious thought to such matters, I will tell you of your mother, or you may read the paper if I am not here. Perhaps my ideas seem peculiar to you, Hester. But all my thought and my effort is to do the best for you. Will you trust and believe in me, Hester?"

"To the end of the world, Aunt Debby. Why should I not? You took me in, a nameless, helpless child, and gave me the very best of your life, even to the name which has always been honored and respected. Don't you think I have known for a long while what sacrifices you have made? That name, Aunt Debby, is as dear to me as to you, and I promise you I will suffer anything before I bring dishonor or shame to it. Hester Palmer Alden. That was the name you loved best — your own mother's. I'm proud of it every time I write it. Trust you!" She leaned her soft cheek against Debby Alden's. "Not trust you, who have done everything for me, and for whom I have done nothing? Oh! Aunt Debby!"

"Done nothing for me!" Debby Alden said the words softly and tenderly, and smiled as she said them. She looked back over the fifteen years and saw what Hester had done for her. She saw herself as she was that morning when the stranger came to the door. She had been an old woman at twenty-five, narrow in her views of life, careless of her language, knowing nothing but the daily routine of housework, with no vital, human interest to draw her from herself. There had come fifteen years of study and discipline with Hester, the friendship of young girls and of women who lived and worked — not worked merely. She was a young girl now at forty, young in spirits, ambitions, and looks. Her horizon had broadened. She could not only see the flowers at her feet, but she had caught the glow of Aurora's rosy fingers on the eastern hilltops, and saw in every shooting star the sacrifice of Berenice.

This came to Debby Alden as she stood

with Hester's cheek pressed to hers. A soft light came to her eyes. She turned, and taking the girl's face between her hands looked at her with a strange new light in her eyes, as she said: "Done nothing for me? I have had fifteen years of love and tenderness from my little girl. Each day has been filled with happiness; my heart has grown greater and my mind keener. The narrow way where I was walking has grown broader and higher ever since the Coming of Hester."

We Four Girls

By MARY G. DARLING 12mo Cloth Illustrated by BERTHA G. DAVIDSON $1.25

"WE FOUR GIRLS" is a bright story of a summer vacation in the country, where these girls were sent for study and recreation. The story has plenty of natural incidents; and a mild romance, in which they are all interested, and of which their teacher is the principal person, gives interest to the tale. They thought it the most delightful summer they ever passed.

A Girl of this Century

By MARY G. DARLING Cloth Illustrated by LILIAN CRAWFORD TRUE $1.25

THE same characters that appear in "We Four Girls" are retained in this story, the interest centering around "Marjorie," the natural leader of the four. She has a brilliant course at Radcliffe, and then comes the world. A romance, long resisted, but worthy in nature and of happy termination, crowns this singularly well-drawn life of the noblest of all princesses — a true American girl.

Beck's Fortune A Story of School and Seminary Life

By ADELE E. THOMPSON Cloth Illustrated $1.25

THE characters in this book seem to live, their remarks are bright and natural, and the incidental humor delightful. The account of Beck's narrow and cheerless early life, her sprightly independence, and unexpected competency that aids her to progress through the medium of seminary life to noble womanhood, is one that mothers can commend to their daughters unreservedly.

For sale by all booksellers or sent postpaid on receipt of price
by the publishers

LOTHROP, LEE & SHEPARD CO., BOSTON

THE GIRL WHO KEPT UP

By MARY McCRAE CUTLER

Illustrated by C. Louise Williams.   12mo.   Cloth. $1.25

This is a strong, wholesome story of achievement. The end of a high school course divides the paths of a boy and girl who have been close friends and keen rivals. The youth is to go to college, while the girl, whose family is in humbler circumstances, must remain at home and help. She sees that her comrade will feel that he is out-growing her, and she determines to and does *keep up* with him in obtaining an education.

"The story is human to the least phase of it, and it is told with such simple force and vivacity that its effect is strong and positive. The pictures of college and home life are true bits of realism. It is an excellent piece of work." — *Bookseller, Newsdealer and Stationer, New York.*

"The story is well told, and is thoroughly helpful in every respect." — *Epworth Herald, Chicago.*

"The telling of the story is attractive, and will be found helpful to all readers." — *The Baptist Union, Chicago.*

"Let us recommend this book for young people for the excellent lesson of honest striving and noble doing that it clearly conveys." — *Boston Courier.*

"It is a healthy and inspiring story." — *Brooklyn Eagle.*

"The tale is full of good lesson for all young people." — *Boston Beacon.*

"The story will be both pleasant and profitable to the youth of both sexes." — *Louisville Courier-Journal.*

For sale by all booksellers, or sent postpaid on receipt of price by

LOTHROP, LEE & SHEPARD CO., Boston

CPSIA information can be obtained at www.ICGtesting.com
Printed in the USA
BVOW021140060112

279983BV00009B/141/P